Julia Pascal

THERESA

A DEAD WOMAN
ON HOLIDAY

THE DYBBUK

OBERON BOOKS
LONDON

This anthology first published in 2000 by Oberon Books Ltd.
(incorporating Absolute Classics)
521 Caledonian Road, London N7 9RH
Tel: 020 7607 3637 / Fax: 020 7607 3629
e-mail: oberon.books@btinternet.com

Theresa first published in the UK by Faber & Faber Ltd, 2000

A catalogue record for this book is available from the British Library.

ISBN 1 84002 094 6

Cover illustration: Andrzej Klimowski

Cover design and typography: Richard Doust

Author photograph: John Nathan

Printed in Great Britain by Antony Rowe Ltd, Reading

Contents

The Holocaust Trilogy
is dedicated to the beloved memory
of my Romanian grandmother, Esther Jacobs,
who taught me that
education is never too heavy to carry around

INTRODUCTION

Julia Pascal

I never decided to write *The Holocaust Trilogy*. The plays *Theresa*, *A Dead Woman on Holiday* and *The Dybbuk* were written individually over a period of three consecutive years and were inspired by stories which seemed to search me out. Jon Harris, then Artistic Director of the New End Theatre, invited me to present *The Holocaust Trilogy* in autumn 1995.

Theresa was provoked by an article I read in the *Observer* in 1989. It described the betrayal of three Jewish women by a British policeman on Guernsey and their subsequent deportation.

Reading this feature changed my life. I was born in Manchester and had a traditional British grammar and comprehensive school education. I tried to be aware of the history of the Second World War yet I had never heard about Jews being expelled from Crown territory. I was brought up with the myth that the British would never collaborate. Indeed what happened on the Channel Islands was a secret history full of shame, guilt and cover-up. Today, nearly a decade after *Theresa*'s premiere, nothing has changed. There are still files on the occupation which the government refuses to release into the public domain. *Theresa* has been seen in England, France, Germany and Switzerland but is banned in Guernsey.

The women betrayed in Guernsey were Theresia Steiner (to give her name its original spelling though her name appears sometimes as Theresa or Therese in the documents I studied), Auguste Spitz and Marianne Grünfeld. The *Observer* revealed how Guernsey Police Inspector W. R. Schulpher forcibly kept Theresa on the island even *before* the Nazis arrived. He was blamed for her fate. Theresia Steiner was murdered in Auschwitz in 1942.

I went to Guernsey to research the play and discovered that it was not only this police inspector who was guilty of events leading to Theresa's murder but the whole of the island government with the honourable exception of Sir Abraham Lainé, who refused to sanction the Nuremberg Laws.

Richard Heaume, director of the Occupation Museum, secreted me with the official documents for four hours. I was not allowed to photocopy the archives and painstakingly copied the obsequious letters from the Bailiff to the *Feldkommandatur* detailing all elements of Jewish life on Guernsey. It made chilling reading and I emerged very disturbed. The guilt was on all levels of island government from the Bailiff down to the police.

I met a woman who had been a nurse with Theresa in Castel Hospital. This 'friend' talked of Theresa's gifts as a piano player. When I asked about Theresa's personality I was told, 'Theresa was very pretty except for her big Jewish nose.' This was 1990: anti Semitism certainly has not disappeared from the island.

When it came to writing the play I knew I was going to direct it and I deliberately decided to cast Ruth Posner who had been a child escapee from the Warsaw Ghetto. It seemed to me that having someone who could transmit this memory of Nazi occupation, through her very presence, was a great bonus to the production. Therefore I created a Theresa Steiner in her fifties though the real Theresa was only 26 when she was gassed in Auschwitz. I was forced to invent her childhood while keeping faithful to what I knew of her life on the island by dramatising the actual documents in what is known as the Informer Scene. Ruth had been a dancer with London Contemporary Dance Theatre and had given up dance for acting. Her experience of being a child in Poland found its way into the text, as did the song expressing innocence before the catastrophe to come. I was keen to use nursery rhyme and children's points of view as a way of showing the destruction of innocence. *Frère Jacques* is a leitmotif for the occupation of sleepwalking France.

Theresa became a performance piece which needed bi- and trilingual European actors. This was to evoke that pre-Holocaust

European Jewish gift of seamlessly flowing from one language to another as my grandparents did.

Stylistically the play is deliberately diverse as a way of showing the fractured universe of exile. I wanted to use nightmare Expressionism in the scenes where Theresa repeatedly relives her betrayal by Lydia; moments of English Music Hall in Theresa's encounters with her several employers; jagged waltz to evoke fragmented Viennese society in the late 1930s and 1960s US Living Theatre techniques to dramatise the easy acceptance of the Nuremberg Laws into Guernsey life. The final moment (when Theresa is taken from Guernsey to her death in Auschwitz) is, of course, impossible to stage. Leaving the image of Theresa juxtaposed against the Nazi officer in a single spotlight while the audience hear the sound of trains mixed with phrases from *The Blue Danube* allows the audience to fill in the final moments of Theresa's life.

The stage play won a prize in the BBC Alfred Bradley Award and was commissioned by BBC Radio 4. It was transmitted in a fine production by Nandita Ghose. By the time I was invited to write this story for BBC Radio 4, I had met Theresa's brother Karl, who escaped the Nazis and found a brief refuge in China. He spoke to me about his sister and told me some of their background. When it came to writing the radio version of Theresa's life, *The Road to Paradise*, I returned Theresa to her real age and gave her a brother whom she adored and was never to see again.

Theresa was banned in Guernsey. However, the Guernsey authorities could not block the airwaves and *The Road to Paradise* (an ironic use of the Nazi description of Auschwitz) was transmitted in 1996 and repeated in 1997.

Meeting Theresa's brother was a moving experience for me. He lives in Canada and was in England to make a first visit to Guernsey. We spoke for some time and I told Karl that I invented Theresa's childhood. Knowing nothing about her family life, I imagined her father had been a musician and a toy manufacturer. To my surprise Karl told me that his father once had a toy factory in Vienna and that it was burnt down!

A Dead Woman on Holiday was inspired by Primo Levi's comment that, 'for a Nazi, a Jew is a dead man on holiday'. The text was born from reading a testimony of those who worked as interpreters at the Nuremberg Trials. I was fascinated to read how individual lives were totally shattered by the act of interpreting the Holocaust. Most of these people had not experienced the *Shoah* directly but were brought in for their language skills. Many broke down. Some fell in love and broke up their marriages. Witness after witness spoke of how the job of transmitting the unthinkable radically changed their lives.

I wanted to use the interpreter as a/the personification of those who, like me, were lucky to have been born too late to experience the death camps but whose lives were obsessed by Hitler's Final Solution. As part of my research I contacted Martha Gellhorn who reported on the Nuremberg Trials. She described returning to her hotel room after hearing the evidence and vomiting.

I also wrote *A Dead Woman on Holiday* to explore the notion of a seemingly impossible love between people of two different cultures. It allowed me to play with notions of language and meaning; areas which I experienced in my Manchester childhood with my Romanian grandparents. They filled my early imagination with the music of many European languages. While I was writing the play, I was living in two languages during my own love affair with a Frenchman, Alain Carpentier, who became my husband in 1994.

The Dybbuk grew out of several journeys to Germany. Germany always seems like a country filled with the ghosts of those who died too early. I wanted to write a play about Jews who were so assimilated they knew almost nothing about their religion. My idea was also to write a piece of late twentieth-century Jewish theatre which connects the Holocaust to S. Anski's great Jewish classic, *The Dybbuk*. In my research I found that Jewish schools still went on in the ghettos and concentration camps: that Jews, who knew they were to die, still continued to educate their children in the knowledge that they would never reach adulthood. The question which haunts me is *why do we still celebrate learning and culture even as the gas chambers are being prepared*? The question is dramatised as the ghetto group feel compelled to complete the story of *The Dybbuk* before they themselves become dybbuks.

I collaborated on the production with German choreographer/performer/designer Thomas Kampe, whose father had been in the *Wehrmacht*. Thomas and I are great admirers of the ninety-year-old Viennese Expressionist dancer Hilde Holger who fled the Nazis in the late 1930s. Her presence and work gave us a sense of the physical, political and cultural flowering of the pre-Hilter years. We felt ourselves her artistic grandchildren and this gave us the inspiration to work together. Thomas created a Dance of Death at the end of *The Dybbuk* which links into this destroyed culture. We were also inspired by the great 1937 Yiddish film *The Dybbuk*, made on the eve of the Holocaust.

We, the children of Jew and Nazi, worked together as an act of cultural reconciliation. Both of us had grown up with a silence around the Holocaust and both of us were actively smashing that silence. It was a very hard journey to make the text into something which would shock, make people laugh, and end in a moment of defiance. Audiences talked about the haunting end when we tried to make five actors represent the six million who died. One by one the actors were told to find a physical expression of resistance. One threw up a pack of cards as if to show that surviving was only a matter of chance. A woman wrapped herself in a *tallus*, a man's prayer shawl, posing several questions at the same time. Another woman walked through tearing her hair. A man laughed silently and manically as if to defy death. Over and over the individuals walked into the light, falling and getting up again and again until their procession suggested the ghosts of all who died and all who are still with us in the gaping grave that is Europe.

The Dybbuk connects to a lost world of Yiddish experience, but in my play I also wanted to take the Jewish mystical wealth and give it a female dimension. When Hanan dies, Esther says *kaddish* for his soul. Traditionally *kaddish*, the prayer for the dead, is only said by the nearest male relative. The inclusion of this prayer will mean little to a non-Jewish audience but for Jewish women it is an act of reclamation. I was forbidden from going to my grandmother Esther Jacobs' funeral in the early 1970s because to Jewish orthodoxy women are considered to be emotionally uncontrollable or, even more worrying, symbols of Eve and the Angel of Death.

I insisted on going to my grandmother's burial: to see her end was an essential part of my human connection to her. Only years later, when I read Bruno Bettelheim, did I realise the importance of the burial ritual on the human psyche. To be denied a grave was a final cruelty the Nazis dealt their victims as they herded them into pits or turned their bodies into smoke.

The act of writing this Trilogy is an attempt to raise some of the questions which surround the Holocaust in the knowledge that there are no answers.

Julia Pascal
London, 2000

The plays were first staged as a trilogy at the New End Theatre on 5 November 1995 with the following cast:

THERESA

THERESA STEINER, Ruth Posner

CASSANDRA, Sarah Finch

JOSEF STEINER, Thomas Kampe

LYDIA ASKEW, Amanda Boxer

WILLIAM SCULPHER, Ian Watts

Director, Julia Pascal
Lighting design, Ian Watts
Design and movement, Thomas Kampe
Original music, Kyla Greenbaum
Sound design, Colin Brown

A DEAD WOMAN ON HOLIDAY

SOPHIA GOLDENBERG, Claire Marchionne

VINCENT WILDING, Jon Harris

DEE DEE CARVER, Hilary Kacser

PAUL CARVER, Kevin Farran

FORMER CONCENTRATION CAMP GUARD, Nickie Goldie

Director, Jon Harris
Lighting design, Ian Watts
Sound design, Colin Brown

THE DYBBUK

ESTHER, Juliet Dante

RACHEL, Nicky Marcus

JAN, Stefan Karsberg

DAVID, Phillipe Smolikowski

NAOMI, Kate Beswick

Director, Julia Pascal
Lighting design, Ian Watts
Design and movement, Thomas Kampe
Original music, Kyla Greenbaum
Sound design, Colin Brown

THERESA

Dedicated to the memory of
Theresia Steiner
who was gassed in
Auschwitz in October 1942

Characters

THERESA STEINER

JOSEF STEINER
her son

LYDIA ASKEW

EDWARD ASKEW
Lydia's husband

LYDIA'S TWO CHILDREN

WILLIAM SCULPHER
a police inspector

HERSCHEL GRYNSZPAN
an anti-Nazi activist

FRANZ SCHÖN

FRENCH STUDENT

GESTAPO OFFICER

CASSANDRA

GUERNSEY GIRL

AUGUSTE SPITZ

NURSES

ENGLISH OFFICIAL

TWO ENGLISH LADIES

FOREIGN OFFICE OFFICIAL

YOUNG JOSEF

MATHILDE
a little girl

WAITRESSES

GUERNSEY WOMEN

GERMAN SOLDIER

MATRON

Theresa was first produced at the Gulbenkian Studio Theatre, Newscastle in March 1990, with the following cast:

THERESA STEINER, Ruth Posner

JOSEF STEINER, Metin Yenal

CASSANDRA/AUGUSTE SPITZ, Monique Burg

LYDIA ASKEW, Kathryn Chambers

Director, Julia Pascal

Design, Penny Fitt

Lighting Design, Ian Watts

Original Music, Kyla Greenbaum

Note:

The play can be performed by four or more actors. The director of each individual production can decide the extent of the doubling that is to take place. Where speeches appear in parallel columns, they are to be spoken simultaneously.

Acknowledgements:

Thanks to the Lisa Ullman Travelling Scholarship Fund which enabled me to travel to Guernsey and research *Theresa*. Thanks also to Thomas Kampe for the German translations, Ruth Posner for the Polish translations and Alain Carpentier for the French translations.

Prologue

THERESA STEINER dances/moves to 'The Blue Danube' by Strauss.

This action to suggest Jews being made to dance.

Memories of a first ball in Vienna. Being in a concentration camp and observing horror. Reaching out to fellow camp inmates: it is a foretaste of the play itself. It also suggests the end of an empire.

The dance should be expressed jaggedly against the sweetness of the Strauss.

Coffee House in Vienna 1938

THERESA: I walk towards the Café de la Bourse on Taborstrasse with its huge windows and sparkling crystal...Does the emperor live there?

THERESA: A man stands in front of the café. It's a cold winter morning. The man is well dressed. He gazes at the window for a minute then strides away. Nonchalantly. He returns casually and looks at the shiny chocolate gateau, the sweet white sponge cakes laced with thick cream. He makes my mouth turn to water; I almost taste the sweetness of the chocolate, the rush of pleasure in my mouth, the gust of life and happiness of black chocolate.

VOICES: *Ein Mann steht vor dem Café. Es ist ein kalter Wintermorgen. Der Mann ist gut angezogen. Er schaut für eine Minute auf das Fenster und geht dann wieder fort. Nonchalant. Lässig kommt er zurück und schaut auf die glänzende Schokoladentorte, den süssweissen Bisquitboden mit dicker Schlagsahne. Das lässt meinen Mund wässrig werden. Ich kann fast die Süsse der Schokolade, die Herzhaftigkeit in meinem Mund, den Genuss und die Freude der schwarzen Schokolade schmecken.*

THERESA: *Nachwilewracam do swojego dziecinstawa Warsawie. Napoleonka. Tak sie to ciastko nazywa. Ja tez tak paczylam przes szby, ale ten sklep nie mial krysztalow to byl maly sklep sprzedajocy zwykle ciasteczka, ale nie dla mine. Moja matka topiedziala nie mozemy sodie na to tozwolic. Wyuij souie to z glowy.*

VOICES: (*Miming a child in Warsaw.*) For a moment I am back in the Warsaw of my childhood. Napoleon. A Napoleon cake. It was called. I stared at the shop window; this shop had no crystal or highly polished glass; it was a small cake shop selling everyday cakes. But not for me. No Napoleon for me. My mother said, 'No we can't afford it. Forget Napoleon.'

THERESA: This man standing outside the Café de la Bourse on *Taborstrasse* is too old to have a mother saying no. She lies beneath marble. He visits her once a week. Or did until recently. He suddenly stands to attention as if in memory of a duel or the war. I imagine medals on his chest under his thick coat. Mine is threadbare. He stands to attention and walks casually into the café. As the doors open a gust of sweetness and warmth mixed with tobacco and perfume clouds out into the street. I follow. He sits at a marble table and a thin

VOICES: *Dieser Mann draussen vor dem Café de la Bourse ist zu alt um eine Mutter zu haben, die 'Nein' sagt. Sie liegt unter Marmor, und er besucht sie einmal in der Woche, hat er zumindest bis vor kurzem. Plötzlich steht er stramm als erinnere er sich an ein Duell, oder den Krieg. Ich stelle mir Medallien an seiner Brust unter seinem dicken Mantel vor. Meiner ist abgewetzt. Er steht stramm und geht dann lässig ins Café. Als die Tür aufgeht entweicht eine süsswarme Wolke von Rauch und Parfüm auf die Strasse. Ich folge dem Mann. Er sitzt an einem*

girl in waitress black and white comes to him. He is presented with a gilded menu on thick cream paper. I can feel its ribbed texture, thicker than the soles of my shoes. Women fill the room with gaiety; their low murmurings betray pleasure as their chocolate-filled mouths move in well-painted bows. A dark red lipstick is in fashion this winter of 1938. The waitress arrives with a *Schwarzwälder Kirschtorte.* How far is it to the Black Forest? She gives him the plate and he spreads a well-starched white white napkin over his knee. She returns with steaming coffee on a silver tray. The thick whipped cream almost flows out of the cup. The carpet is thick pile. I don't notice my thin shoes now. Silk curtains adorn the walls, draping them like at the theatre. Most of the well-dressed men and women are sipping chocolate and delicately pushing small portions of *petits fours*

Marmortisch und ein dünnes Madel im weissen Bedienungskostüm kommt zu ihm. Er bekommt ein vergoldetes Besteck auf dickem Cremepapier. Ich kann dessen gerippte Oberfläche, die dicker als die Sohlen meiner Schuhe ist, fast spüren. Frauen füllen den Raum mit Heiterkeit. Ihr tiefes Gemurmel verschweigt den Genuss während sich ihre Schokoladen gefüllten Münder in schönbemalten Bögen bewegen. Man trägt dunklen Lippenstift im Winter 1938. Die Bedienung kommt mit einer Schwarzwälder Kirschtorte. Sie gibt ihm einen Teller und er breitet eine gut gestärkte, weisse Serviette uber seine Knie. Sie kommt mit dampfendem Kaffee auf einem Silbertablet. Die dicke weisse Sahne fliesst fast aus der Tasse heraus. Der Teppich ist dick und weich. Ich bemerke jetzt meine dünnen Schuhe garnicht mehr. Seidene Vorhänge verkleiden die Wände, verkleiden sie wie ein Theater. Die meisten der gut angezogenen Männer und Frauen trinken

through their rouged lips or beneath well-trimmed moustaches. He pushes aside half of the Black Forest cherry cake. I examine it from across the café. I can almost taste the thick cream, the soft dark sponge, the red *kirsch* and the kick of the alcohol. He pushes it aside as if he has had enough; it is the studied effect of a man playing the millionaire. He takes out a newspaper, crosses his legs and casually lights a cigarette, inhaling it deeply into the base of his lungs. As he does, he looks out of the highly polished crystal glass window. SA men are beating Jews in the cold morning. They are having great fun with an elderly couple of Jewish workers pushed onto their hands and knees, forced to scrub the street. A group of pretty prostitutes are screaming with laughter at the pair old enough to be their grandparents. 'Give them some fresh water.' And a bucket of piss and shit is hurled at the Jews. The man in the café

Schokolade und schieben genüsslich kleine Stückchen petits fours unter ihre gut gestutzten Schnurrbärte. Er schiebt die Hälfte der Schwarzwälder Kirschtorte zur Seite. Ich betrachte sie von gegenüber. Ich kann fast die dicke Sahne, den dunkeln weichen Boden, die roten Kirschen und den Schuss Alkohol schmecken. Er schiebt sie zu Seite als habe er genug; das ist der einstudierte Effekt eines gespielten Millionärs. Er nimmt sich ein Zeitung, schlägt die Beine übernander und zuendet sich lässig eine Zigarette an, deren Rauch er tief in die Lungen inhaliert. Während er das tut, schaut er aus dem hochpoliertem Kristallfenster. SA Männer haben ihren Spass mit einem älteren jüdischem Paar, die auf den Händen und Füssen die Strasse schrubben. Eine Gruppe hübscher Nutten schaut vergnugt zu dem Paar, welches leicht deren Grosseltern sein könnten. 'Give them some fresh water.' Und ein Eimer Pisse und Scheisse wird auf die Juden geworfen. Der Mann im Café dreht sich weg. Er ist weiss. Schnell isst er seine Torte auf. Zu schnell. Sie

turns his face away.
He is white. He eats his
cake quickly. Too quickly.
It was meant to last all
morning. Now it's gone.
The waitress is standing
beside the marble-
topped table with the
bill. He puts his hand in
his pocket for the three
thousand. His last few
schillings change are for
her tip. She smiles. His
last banknote on a cake
and a coffee. He leaves
the crystal glass, marble-
tabled, thick-pile carpet,
silk-curtained Café de la
Bourse and walks out
from the perfumed,
sweet, chocolate-filled air
into the cold winter
morning. Turning away
from the raucous
laughter of the prostitutes
and away from the men
in uniforms, he looks
down onto the heads of
the old couple; their
veined hands scrubbing
the street. He stares in
frozen fascination while
the well-dressed men
and women in the café
continue sipping their
chocolate and ordering
another cake.

*sollte doch den ganzen
Morgen halten. Jetzt ist
sie alle. Die Bedienung
steht schon mit der
Rechnung am
Marmortisch. Er steckt
seine Hand in die Tasche
für die drei tausend.
Seine letzten paar Schillinge
sind für's Trinkgeld.
Sie lächelt. Seine letzte
Banknote, für ein Stück
Torte und ein Tässerl
Kaffee. Er verlässt
das kristallgläserne,
marmorbetischte Café de
la Bourse in der
Taborstrasse mit dickem
Teppich und seidenen
Vorhängen, und geht
hinaus und Parfüm
gefüllten Luft in den kalten
Wintermorgen. Während
er sich von den Nutten
und den Uniformierten
wegdreht, schaut er auf
die Köpfe des älterne
Paares, deren faltigen
Hände die Strasse
schrubben. Er starrt in
erfrorener Faszination.
Die gut angezogenen
Männer und Frauen im
Café trinken weiter
Schokolade und bestellen
'Noch eine Torte'.*

JULIA PASCAL

Vienna Music Conservatory 1938
The Lesson

THERESA gives her final lecture to her students in Vienna Conservatory.

THERESA: Today we were to continue our discussion on
Schönberg. We will not be doing that because today is
my last day as Professor of Music in this Conservatory.
The Nazis have forbidden Jews to teach gentiles. We
Jewish teachers must disappear.
As undergraduates you have the right to expect the
broadest education. We are all the inheritors of those
who question our bourgeois, conservative society. New
forms are being expressed. James Joyce, Sigmund
Freud, Alban Berg, Stravinsky, Schönberg, Weill, Eisler
are a few who challenge the old order. These men are
despised by the Nazis. Hitler sees them as 'degenerate'.
But what is degenerate? To him all Jews are degenerate.
To him Bolsheviks, Communists and Socialists are
degenerate. They are taking these so-called degenerates
to Dachau.
When I was a young woman I used to stare in fascination
at my own hair. Sometimes a strand of black, coarse, frizzy
hair would appear. My hair always had to be tamed when
I was a child and there were hours spent by mother
brushing it in some kind of order. I used to cry because it
wasn't smooth and fair like other girls'. It was like a
gypsy's, they would say. Or an African's.
The Nazi ideal is to make people with hair and features
which conform to the Aryan stereotype. In this new
world there will be no room for our differences. Our
quirky individual differences. Beauty will be made to
order.
They are already killing their own old people and
they want to kill all Jews, gypsies, Communists and
homosexuals – anyone who doesn't fit into the myth
of the Super Race.
Up to now you've been lucky enough to taste the
flavour of these new languages. You've listened to
Schönberg, read Sigmund Freud, seen the works of

Erwin Piscator and Georg Grosz. Whether you accept the Nazi art is up to you. But you will have tasted the forbidden.

Whatever happens to me, you must go on. Remember our discussions and whisper them to your friends. Seal them in your brain cells until this order is over.

(*Pause.*)

I wish you long life.

FRENCH STUDENT: May I speak to you, Frau Doktor Steiner?

THERESA: Yes, of course.

FRENCH STUDENT: My name is Esther Jacobson. I am from Paris. I heard your talk.

THERESA: You are not one of my students, are you?

FRENCH STUDENT: No. I am studying Fine Art. Or rather, I was studying.

THERESA: Are you a Jew?

FRENCH STUDENT: I have a Jewish grandmother.

THERESA: You could go back to France.

FRENCH STUDENT: And if the Nazis invade France there will be plenty of 'righteous Christians' who will be delighted to talk about my grandmother.

THERESA: What will you do?

FRENCH STUDENT: I have to go to Palestine. It's the only place we can be safe.

THERESA: And if the British don't allow you in?

FRENCH STUDENT: I'll get in illegally. Come with us?

THERESA: I can't do that.

FRENCH STUDENT: Why not?

THERESA: I don't speak Hebrew.

FRENCH STUDENT: You'll learn.

THERESA: There is more to it than the language. I am a European. I am not a Zionist. Europe is my home. We are Austrians. My husband fought in the last war. My parents came from Poland. I speak Polish, German, French and English. These are my languages. I am a European. Why should I be pushed off this continent because one man says so? I have the right to live here. Why should I be forced to live in the Middle East?

FRENCH STUDENT: How will you survive?

THERESA: I will go to London. I have made arrangements.
I will go to London with my son. We will wait until this is
over. We will start again.

FRENCH STUDENT: Excuse me but aren't you being
a little naïve?

THERESA: Naïve? (*Beat.*) Maybe you are right. I have
become a 'Christian' Jew. I've got used to a little bit of
anti-Semitism every day. A remark about a large nose,
a dark appearance, love of money. Killer of Jesus.

FRENCH STUDENT: Maybe I'll see you next year? In
Jerusalem?

THERESA: Maybe.

Kristallnacht
The Night of the Broken Glass
November 9 1938

*Scene opens with THERESA and JOSEF moving to Krysztof
Penderezcki's 'To the Memory of the Victims of Hiroshima'.*

*Both are in isolated spots. The mood is of terror and isolation as if to
express the experience of Kristallnacht.*

Lights up on whole stage.

NARRATOR: Kristallnacht. November 1938.
In Paris a young Jew kills a Nazi diplomat.

HERSCHEL: The Nazis. They killed my parents. Now it's
your turn.

CASSANDRA: The little Austrian with a moustache who
failed as a painter was delighted. It was the perfect
excuse.

THERESA: Kristallnacht.

NARRATOR: The Night of the Broken Glass.

THERESA: Kristallnacht.

CASSANDRA: Listen, Jews, you have the warnings. Go. Get
away from the little man with the moustache. He wants
to break your bones like glass. He wants to burn your

flesh. And take the gold from your teeth. And if you have no gold, he will take your teeth. He will take your skin and make lampshades. He will make a mountain of hair. A mountain of hair. A mountain of hair. And teeth and glasses and shoes and dresses and jackets and trousers. And one day, in the future, a young woman will go into a second-hand shop in Heidelberg and she will look at the shirts hanging on the rail and she will see names like Goldberg, like Friedmann, like Jacobson, like Steiner.

THERESA: Like Steiner?

CASSANDRA: Josef Steiner.

THERESA: I sewed the name in his shirts.

CASSANDRA: Josef Steiner sewed into the collar of a shirt made for dancing in...But who will remember these men? These women? Murdered by the little man in the moustache?

HERSCHEL: You killed my parents.

CASSANDRA: Today they'll say, 'It never happened.' 'How could it happen?' 'Who would do such a thing?' (*Becoming a French anti-Semite.*) '*C'est une invention juive!*'

HERSCHEL: (*Becoming a neo-Nazi.*) '*Dass ist eine jüdische Erfindung.*'

THERESA: (*Momentarily breaking character to express Polish anti-Semitic view.*) *Wynalazek zydowski*!

The Departure

Spotlight on THERESA only. She sings a childhood Polish song.

THERESA: *Cherwone jab utzko*
przekrojone ma krzyi
Czemu ty dziewczyno
Krzywo ma mnic patszysz
gesi za woda
kaczki za wodq
vciekaj dziewczymo
bo cic poboda
ja ci buzi dam

ty mi buzi dasz
ja cic mic wydam i ty mnic nic wydasz
ja za woda, ty za woda
Jakzi ja ci buzi podam
podam ci jz, na lystczku
czekaj, czekaj kochaneczku!
(*As the music gets lighter and jollier, other actors throw a case, a hat and a coat at THERESA to break the mood. Train sounds.*
Lights up on THERESA and JOSEF. Both actors are looking out. THERESA is manically folding and unfolding a coat to be packed. JOSEF is closing his jacket, only he keeps buttoning it the wrong way.)

THERESA: We've got to go. Can't you see what's happening?

JOSEF: Yes, I'll follow. I can't go yet. I've got too many people to see. I've got to finish everything. The newspaper...

THERESA: You've no job. You've no family apart from me. What is there to stay for?

JOSEF: It'll soon pass. It's just a temporary situation. It won't last. I can't speak English.

THERESA: You'll learn quickly. I've got visas for both of us.

JOSEF: Give me mine, Mother. I'll follow. Go find somewhere comfortable for us. You can be a cook and I'll be an English butler. Won't I look good in a butler's uniform?

THERESA: Don't make me go alone.
(*Train sounds.*)

The Journey to England from Vienna

Train sounds. Vienna station.

THERESA: They put a J in my passport. For Jew.

1ST MAN: *Jude.* If Jesus wanted a passport, they would stamp a J in his.

VIENNESE JEWISH WOMAN: (*To unseeing crowds on platform.*) Take my baby. Take her with you. I can't get a visa. I can't get a job in England. 'No maids. No cooks. No nannies. No cleaners.'

ENGLISH OFFICIAL: No German teachers, definitely no German teachers.

VIENNESE JEWISH WOMAN: Take my baby. Let her live. There's an address. An agency. Good people will take her. Will find her new parents. I beg you let her live.

(*THERESA opens her arms and takes the BABY.*)

MALE ACTOR: (*Sings German nursery rhyme.*)
Widele Wedele
Hinterm Städtele
Hält der Bettelmann Hochzeit
Tanzt das Läusele
Pfeift das Mäusele
Schlagt das Igele
Trommel.
(*By now everyone has placards around their necks with 'Wien nach London' for the Kindertransport – except THERESA. Train sounds continue.*)

THERESA: Holland! People shouting, giving us sandwiches and chocolates. London.

(*Train sounds stop.*)

Men in bowlers. Umbrellas. I register as an alien.

ENGLISH OFFICIAL: Alien.

THERESA: I have only ten marks. It's all they allowed me to take.

1ST ENGLISH LADY: You can work for me. You can't use the hoover. Use the brush and pan. Servants only break the hoover. Believe you me.

ENGLISH OFFICIAL: Now you have to register with me every week. Remember you are an alien. If you move towns you have to register. If you move districts, even districts here in London, you have to register. You have to register.

1ST ENGLISH LADY: If you want to eat in the house then you have to eat in the scullery.

(*Time passes. Stylised movement.*)

What are these crumbs? You've been eating your breakfast in my kitchen, haven't you?

THERESA: Please, I have to go out. Friday. My day off. I have to go to the station. To see if my son is arriving. From Vienna. I must meet the train.

1ST ENGLISH LADY: No, you've been eating in my kitchen. No more days off for a month. Subject closed.

THERESA: Excuse me, Madam...

1ST ENGLISH LADY: Don't!

(*Scene cuts to Liverpool Street station, London.*)

VOICE OVER: The train arriving at Platform Four is the connection from Vienna via the Hook of Holland and Harwich.

(*THERESA sees someone she thinks is JOSEF. As she reaches out to him he moves away singing 'Hänschen Klein'.*)

BOY: *Hänschen klein*

Ging allein

In die weite Welt allein

Stock und hut

Steht ihm gut

Ist auch wohl Gemut.

(*Scene cuts back.*)

1ST ENGLISH LADY: I want to talk to you, Steiner. You deliberately went against my orders and went to the station. You're sacked.

THERESA: (*As if to police.*) Change of address. Theresa Steiner. Domestic. Leaving London. Going to Wiltshire. To work. As a domestic.

2ND ENGLISH LADY: Theresa Steiner?
I know we spoke about your coming here. I had a phone call from your previous employer this morning, Mrs Powell. A very respectable lady. She said you are unreliable and disobedient. She said you went out directly against her wishes.

THERESA: My son. I had to see if he was coming. From Vienna. My day off.

2ND ENGLISH LADY: I don't know why they just don't intern the whole bloody lot of you.

The Interview

This scene starts with THERESA walking from door to door in search of work. Each door is slammed in her face. Finally she comes to the house of LYDIA ASKEW. Set against Noël Coward's 'Don't Let's Be Beastly to the Germans'.

THERESA: Mrs Askew?

LYDIA: Yes?

THERESA: It's about the advertisement in *The Lady*.

LYDIA: Oh. I was expecting a younger woman. (*Pause.*) Oh excuse me. How rude. Do come in.

THERESA: Thank you.

LYDIA: Tea?

THERESA: Thank you.

LYDIA: With milk?

THERESA: Yes please.

LYDIA: How long have you been in this country?

THERESA: Three weeks.

LYDIA: I see. Not long is it?

THERESA: No, not long.

LYDIA: And how do you find the English?

THERESA: (*Pause.*) Very polite.

LYDIA: But cold?

THERESA: Yes, how did you know?

LYDIA: I didn't know I was going to say that.

THERESA: I think you read my mind.

LYDIA: Have something to eat. A cake? It's a good Battenberg.

THERESA: Battenberg? A royal cake?

LYDIA: (*Awkward.*) Yes, I suppose you could say that.

THERESA: It's very colourful.

LYDIA: Now where were we?

THERESA: The job.

LYDIA: Yes, well, as I said, I really was looking for a younger woman. I can't pay much.

THERESA: That doesn't matter.

LYDIA: Have you any experience as a nanny?

THERESA: I'm a Professor of Music at Vienna Conservatory.

LYDIA: I could tell that you were something else, something higher in the world.

THERESA: I have experience with children.

LYDIA: Oh?

THERESA: I have a son.

LYDIA: A son. I hadn't realised you were married.

THERESA: I am a widow. My husband died in the First War.

LYDIA: So did my father.

(*Pause.*)

But on the other side of course.

THERESA: Of course.

LYDIA: And you are a German.

THERESA: An Austrian.

LYDIA: I'm sorry, an Austrian...

THERESA: I am also a Jew...that's why I had to leave. My family came to Vienna when I was a child. From Warsaw. From Poland.

LYDIA: Poor Poland.

THERESA: Yes, poor Poland.

LYDIA: Was your family rich?

THERESA: Not all Jews are rich.

LYDIA: I'm sorry, that's very crass.

THERESA: They were musicians. They were not rich.

LYDIA: And you have a son you say?

THERESA: Yes.

LYDIA: And where is he now?

THERESA: He's still in Vienna.

(*Pause.*)

LYDIA: Would you like to meet my little girl?

THERESA: Oh yes please.

(*Cut to CHILDREN. LITTLE BOY sings 'Ring a Ring a Roses' in German – a clapping game with the LITTLE GIRL.*)

LITTLE BOY: *Ringe, Ringe, Reihe*
wir sind unser Dreihe
sitzen unterm Holderbusch
machen alle Husch husch husch.

(*THERESA joins in. The LITTLE BOY disappears. The LITTLE GIRL is left. THERESA brings the LITTLE GIRL centre stage to have her hair brushed by LYDIA. The LITTLE GIRL carries a bald Victorian doll.*)

Lydia's Story

Although this is a monologue the action includes everyone. Chopin's
Opus 27 No. 2 in D Flat is used against the first half.

LYDIA: I can talk to you. I don't know why I feel this but
I know I can talk to you. Maybe it's because you're not
from this country. You know nothing about me or where
I come from. I liked you instinctively. *Simpatico*. Isn't
that what they call it? Or maybe because you're older.
You could almost be my mother. Hardly. My mother's
not like you. She's not one for talking. Not about
anything serious. Not that I ever saw much of my mother
when I was a child. They sent me away. My sister Joy and
I were both sent away to boarding school. Different
boarding schools. We were both without friends. That
was the idea. To make us independent. To make us
'nicely behaved young women'. Make nicely behaved
young women out of us. Is that what I am?
(*Pause.*)
Yes, I suppose it is.
And then after school came the dances, the presentations,
the long dresses and the correct shoes. Everything had
to be so correct. I hated it. And all those young men who
kept calling at the house. Pale-faced men with stammers
and 'good prospects'. How I hated them. Was this all
life had to offer? 'Yes,' Mother said. 'Yes,' Father said
and disappeared into a bottle of whisky. We had maids.
They were fun. Irish girls with stories about fairies who
stole babies. I liked those. They were always fun. But
Mother wanted to get rid of them. They used to take me
to church with them. Incense, I remember. When
Mother found out she gave them the sack. So there was
never anyone to talk to. Not really talk. There was only
Mother and Father and Silence Is Golden and Little
Girls Should Be Seen And Not Heard.
(*The LITTLE GIRL gets up with her doll and leaves space.*
The same actress re-enters with a hat and becomes the OTHER
WOMAN. The MALE ACTOR plays Edward Askew. He lifts
LYDIA and flirts with the OTHER WOMAN.)

And then I met Him. Edward. Edward Askew. His father and my father were great friends. Edward had always been away at school and I'd played with him occasionally in the holidays. But I never thought he'd want to marry me. He was too tall. Too good-looking. Too everything. I heard he'd been with lots of women; he told jokes, laughed a lot. But he came and took me out. To the cinema. To the seaside. We walked on Brighton Pier and the wind was so high my skirt flew up. He laughed and said I had good legs. I blushed. Then he said he wanted to marry me. I laughed. I thought he was mocking me.

We got married. Five years ago. That first night I was scared. He was sweet with me. Very sweet. And then the babies came quickly. He seemed to get bored. Stayed out late. And if we did go out together I saw his eyes follow others. I felt small and insignificant, as if I didn't matter any more. He wanted to be with others. I knew that. And at night, when he came in late, he turned away from me in the bed and I felt such a pain in my stomach, it was worse than the pain of a child's birth. For hours I lay awake beside him, wanting him to touch me but knowing that somehow everything had changed. What was it? Was it the babies? I didn't know. And when the war came, he volunteered immediately.

With relief, I thought. Relief to get away from me and back to a life of his own. Like school with the boys.

I sometimes think maybe he'll die and then I won't have to watch him watching all those others. It's a terrible thought but I can't help it and then I just long for him, long for how it was before the babies, when we walked on the pier and he held my hand. And every time the post comes I wonder if it'll be a letter, a letter telling me the worst, or is it the best? (*Beat.*)

His death would free me!

I wouldn't have to put up with the thought of other women any more; his eyes on their breasts, their hips, their legs. (*Beat.*)

Are all men like that? Do they all make us feel so small?

Theresa's Story

THERESA: My father worked in a toy factory. I had
wonderful toys for Christmas. In school we all wore
aprons. My mother made me special aprons. Every night
my mother darned our stockings. And Father's socks.
She darned the socks and supervised us in our
homework.
There was always music in the house. Mother sang
songs. We had gas light. We sat around the stove to keep
warm and sang songs. My grandfather came from
Bavaria. He told us stories of Hansel and Gretel.
(*THERESA and the actor playing YOUNG JOSEF sing
'Hansel and Gretel' in German.*)

THERESA/JOSEF: *Hänsel und Gretel verirrten sich im Wald
es war so finster und auch so bitter kalt
sie kamen an ein Häuschen
von Pfefferkuchen fein
Wer mag der Herr wohl
von diesem Häuschen sein?*

THERESA: He read us fairytales. Hans Christian Andersen.
The Brothers Grimm. I hated dolls. They were so cold.
They sent me to the hospital because of the measles. It
was so lonely. Grandmother came and brought me dolls.
But I didn't want them. Where was my mother? They
put us in high beds because there weren't enough cots.
And then they made me go on the potty. Sister said, 'I'll
put the potty in the bed and then you can "go" in the
bed.' I said, 'No, I'll wait till I go home.'
When the war came I was always so hungry. By then I was
married. Like you, I was only a short time married. He
was killed in 1917.
When I was a little girl I taught myself to read. When
I went to school it was a shock. I sat in the second place.
The first in the class was Mathilde Liebich. She was the
daughter of the headmaster. She was supposed to sit
next to me. First was the first and the second was me.
But she wouldn't.

MATHILDE: I don't want to sit next to you because you're a Jew. I don't like Jews.

THERESA: Then I didn't want to be second to her. I wanted to be third.

(*Pause.*)

My son. He promised to follow me. I got a visa each. I got invitations. He could be a butler in Kensington. I was to be the maid.

(*Music for the Savoy Hotel links into next scene.*)

The Savoy Hotel, London 1939

The Savoy lounge where German émigrés go to hear the music.

Two WAITRESSES get ready and then set up chairs. The scene should have elements of absurdism. THERESA enters and sees a young man standing with his back to her.

THERESA: Josef?

(*The young man turns.*)

FRANZ: Sit please.

Franz.

THERESA: Franz?

FRANZ: Franz Schön. Berlin.

THERESA: Theresa. Steiner. *Wien.* Vienna.

(*FRANZ extends his hand and becomes very English.*)

FRANZ: How do you do?

THERESA: Thank you very much.

FRANZ: Nice weather.

THERESA: How long did you take to learn English?

FRANZ: From going to the cinema.

THERESA: Ah.

FRANZ: Coffee? Tea?

THERESA: Coffee. Yes. Coffee.

FRANZ: Coffee in England is awful.

(*FRANZ beckons to WAITRESSES. They ignore him. This happens several times.*)

FRANZ: They never see me.

THERESA: People must be going to the opera. In Vienna.

(*WAITRESSES bring coffee.*)

FRANZ: The coffee. So thin. Cake?

THERESA: No thank you.

FRANZ: I understand. It's not *Sachertorte.*

THERESA: What did you do in Berlin?

FRANZ: Professor. Architecture. Berlin University. You?

THERESA: Professor of Music. Vienna Conservatory.

FRANZ: *Erste Stock. Zweiter Stock. Dritter Stock. Vierter Stock. Ja*
    Madam. Nein Madam. Bitte schön, danke schön.
    (*Beat.*) I work the lift here. This is my tea break. I come
    for the music. The memories of home.

THERESA: You like England?

FRANZ: Yes. Yes. Yes. (*Beat.*) You?

THERESA: I'm getting used to it. How old are you?

FRANZ: Thirty-one.

THERESA: I have a son in Vienna.

FRANZ: How old is he?

THERESA: Also thirty-one.

FRANZ: A Professor of Architecture?

THERESA: No.
    (*Pause.*)
    Franz.

FRANZ: Herr Professor Franz Schön.

THERESA: Nice name — Franz.

FRANZ: What's your son's name?
    (*Pause.*)

THERESA: Do you have a cigarette?

FRANZ: Bad for health. Your son?

THERESA: Let's listen to the music, shall we.

FRANZ: I come here every day to listen to the music.

THERESA: I have to go soon. I've got a job. Nanny.

FRANZ: Between five and five thirty every day. My tea
    break. In this place.

THERESA: Between five and five thirty.

FRANZ: Or in the lift. Number seven. It's the best lift.
    (*THERESA gets up. FRANZ kisses her hand.*)

THERESA: Goodbye, Herr Professor.

FRANZ: *Auf Wiedersehen.* Don't forget. Lift number seven.
    (*THERESA exits. FRANZ is thrown the bell boy's hat by a*
    WAITRESS. He dusts it and places it on his head. Hold his
    humiliation for a moment then scene changes.)

Lydia's House

Voice-over: Chamberlain's declaration of the beginning of the war.

THERESA has stylised movement during the voice over. LYDIA is preparing the LITTLE GIRL's clothes.

LYDIA: Go. We've got to go.

THERESA: Go? Go where? Where can we go?

LYDIA: I can't risk it. The children. What happens when they start bombing London?

THERESA: But where can we go? I'm a Jew. I can't just go anywhere. I'm an 'enemy alien'. I have to report, don't forget.

LYDIA: We'll go to the Channel Islands. My brother's wife lives there.

THERESA: Where are the Channel Islands?

LYDIA: Near France.

THERESA: Near France. Is that safe?

LYDIA: Don't worry, they're safe. They're British. We'll all be safe there.

(*Sound of ship's horn.*)

Guernsey, September 1940

Two GUERNSEY WOMEN and a British police inspector, WILLIAM SCULPHER. Same character throughout the rest of the play.

NARRATOR: Guernsey.

SCULPHER: Theresa Steiner. Registration. Now you are on the island of Guernsey you must report to me. And surrender your passport.

1ST GUERNSEY WOMAN: Who is that woman?

SCULPHER: An outsider.

2ND GUERNSEY WOMAN: A Jew.

1ST GUERNSEY WOMAN: They say the Germans are getting closer to Paris.

SCULPHER: They've occupied Paris.

1ST GUERNSEY WOMAN: Paris! Will we have to evacuate?

2ND GUERNSEY WOMAN: No. I'm staying here.

1ST GUERNSEY WOMAN: The army will save us.

SCULPHER: Don't be silly — the army's all left.

2ND GUERNSEY WOMAN: We don't have to go do we?

1ST GUERNSEY WOMAN: I don't want to go to England.

SCULPHER: The Guernsey authorities have said we'll be safe with the Germans. They won't hurt us.

Stranded

Stylised movement from THERESA and LYDIA during this voice-over.

VOICE-OVER: People of Guernsey. Evacuation boats will be ready for boarding immediately. The Germans are expected any day. British military personnel have been evacuated from the island. No danger is expected to the local community but anyone wishing to leave the island for England Southampton must register immediately.

LYDIA. I've got to go. I need tickets for two adults and two children.

SCULPHER: You can go, madam. This lady stays.

LYDIA: You don't seem to understand, Inspector. She is my nanny. She's been living with me in London for over a year. She's my responsibility.

SCULPHER: Theresa Steiner was born in Vienna. She has a J stamped in her passport. That means she's a Jew.

THERESA: Yes. I am a Jew.

SCULPHER: Austria has been annexed by the Germans. So this woman belongs to the Germans. They'll decide what to do with her. In the meantime she can work as a nurse. She'll be useful here.

LYDIA. But the Germans haven't invaded.

SCULPHER: Yet.

LYDIA: You can let her go.

SCULPHER: She stays with me. Subject closed.
   (*Sound of ship's horn.*)

LYDIA: Theresa. Please forgive me. I have to get back. For the children's sake.
   (*THERESA hugs LYDIA. LYDIA accepts the moment then pushes THERESA away. Scene then shifts to surreal repeats with different lighting effects.*)

Theresa's Nightmare

LYDIA: I need tickets.
SCULPHER: This lady stays.
LYDIA: My responsibility.
SCULPHER: Vienna.
  J.
  Jew.
THERESA: Yes. I am a Jew. I am a Jew. I am a Jew.
SCULPHER: Belongs to Germans.
LYDIA: Haven't invaded.
SCULPHER: She stays with me.
LYDIA: Forgive.

Replay 2

LYDIA: I need tickets.
SCULPHER: This lady stays.
LYDIA: My responsibility.
SCULPHER: Vienna.
  J.
  Jew.
THERESA: Yes. I am a Jew. I am a Jew. I am a Jew.
SCULPHER: Belongs to Germans.
LYDIA: Haven't invaded.
SCULPHER: She stays with me.
LYDIA: Forgive.

Replay 3

LYDIA: I need tickets.
SCULPHER: This lady stays.
LYDIA: My responsibility.
SCULPHER: Vienna.
  J.
  Jew.
THERESA: Yes. I am a Jew. I am a Jew. I am a Jew.
SCULPHER: Belongs to Germans.
LYDIA: Haven't invaded.

SCULPHER: She stays with me.
LYDIA: Forgive.

Replay 4

LYDIA: I need tickets.
SCULPHER: This lady stays.
LYDIA: My responsibility.
SCULPHER: Vienna.
    J.
    Jew.
THERESA: Yes. I am a Jew. I am a Jew. I am a Jew.
SCULPHER: Belongs to Germans.
LYDIA: Haven't invaded.
SCULPHER: She stays with me.
LYDIA: Forgive.

Replay 5

LYDIA: I need tickets.
SCULPHER: This lady stays.
LYDIA: My responsibility.
SCULPHER: Vienna.
    J.
    Jew.
THERESA: Yes. I am a Jew. I am a Jew. I am a Jew.
SCULPHER: Belongs to Germans.
LYDIA: Haven't invaded.
SCULPHER: She stays with me.
LYDIA: Forgive.

Replay 6

LYDIA: I need tickets.
SCULPHER: This lady stays.
LYDIA: My responsibility.
SCULPHER: Vienna.
    J.
    Jew.

THERESA: Yes. I am a Jew. I am a Jew. I am a Jew.
SCULPHER: Belongs to Germans.
LYDIA: Haven't invaded.
SCULPHER: She stays with me.
LYDIA: Forgive.
Forgive.
Forgive.

The Collaboration

NARRATOR: The swastika flies from the Arc de Triomphe.
France continues to sleep.
(*She sings 'Je Te Veux', music by Erik Satie and lyrics by Henry Pacory. She dances with a Gestapo hat. The song symbolises France's collaboration with the Nazis. To be performed with irony.*)

The Occupation of France

An ACTOR takes a simple movement of being stroked on the back of the neck as a child. He sings 'Frère Jacques' in French. Gradually the movement becomes repeated. The stroking turns out to be a beating by an oppressor. He gradually changes from joyful child to victim of Nazi. His movement and sound gradually become more and more anguished. His 'Frère Jacques' changes into 'Bruder Jakob'.

Another ACTOR starts as a little girl at a concert. Gradually her 'Frère Jacques' becomes 'Bruder Jakob' as she is forced to sing in German. Her movement gradually changes. The little girl is kicked in the leg, forcing her into a cancan step which becomes a goose-step.

Frère Jacques	*Bruder Jakob*
Dormez vous?	*Schläfst du noch?*
Dormez vous?	*Schläfst du noch?*
Sonnez les matines	*Hörst du nicht die Glocke?*
Sonnez les matines	*Hörst du nicht die Glocke?*
Ding dang dong	*Ding dang dong*
Ding dang dong	*Ding dang dong*

The Informer Scene, Guernsey 1940-2

1ST NURSE: I'll see you at the end of the war. In 1943.
In London. Under Big Ben. The war's bound to be over
in a year.

THERESA: (*In nurse's hat.*) Come on, let's make the beds.
Let's have a race, see who can make the beds quickest.
I can do one in three minutes.

SCULPHER: We're making a list of Jewish people on
the island.

2ND NARRATOR: Do you know who the Jews are?

1ST NURSE: Yes, they're people from Palestine like Theresa
here.

2ND NARRATOR: Do you like Theresa?

1ST NURSE: Yes, she's pretty. But it's a pity her appearance
is spoilt by her big Jewish nose.

SCULPHER: Theresa Steiner. You have to report to us
every week.

THERESA: My son. In Vienna. I was waiting for him to
come. Do you know what happened to my son?

1ST NURSE: It'll soon be Budelot Night. Where will I get
fireworks now?

THERESA: What's that?

2ND NARRATOR: The end of the year. *Bout de l'an.*

1ST NURSE: When we burn the Guy.

THERESA: Burn the guy?

1ST NARRATOR: In the Nazi concentration camp on the
British island of Alderney the prisoners arrive in the
uniforms of 1941.

2ND NARRATOR: They still wear them in 1942.

1ST NARRATOR: When a man dies because he is beaten to
death in Alderney others cluster around him to inherit
his tatters.
A carrot is thrown from a window by a cook.

2ND NARRATOR: A Russian slave worker sees it and runs
for it.

1ST NARRATOR: A Nazi watching him takes out his whip
and lashes the Russian on the face, on the head, on the
body, until he is nothing but a red thing, a hideous
thing, a poor, starving dead thing.

2ND NARRATOR: *Ils prennent les combattants juifs français de la résistance et les enferment dans un tunnel. Ils les enfermerons dans un tunnel pour les priver d'air. Au dessus du tunnel les prostituées françaises prennent un bain de soleil à Alderney.*

1ST NARRATOR: They take the Jewish French Resistance fighters and lock them in a tunnel. They will lock them in a tunnel to starve them of air. Above the tunnel the French prostitutes sunbathe. In Alderney.

2ND NARRATOR: Some Guernsey women share their beds and open their legs to the Nazis.

1ST NARRATOR: 'Jerrybags', the locals call them.
(*Sound of marching songs.*)

1ST NURSE: I hear their marching songs. So many good-looking Germans. So tall, so young, so handsome.

1ST NARRATOR: Who can blame the women for falling for them?

1ST NURSE: Who can blame them for wanting a little bit extra? (*To GESTAPO OFFICER.*) Herr Kommandant. My brother is breaking the law. He's got a radio.

2ND NARRATOR: That woman eats well tonight.

THERESA: What about my son? Have you any news of my son? He was to come and find me. I've no letters, no message, no nothing.

GESTAPO OFFICER: Jews are forbidden to go to the cafés, cinemas, museums, weekly markets.

SCULPHER: Libraries, sports places, family bathing places.

THERESA: The *Guernsey Evening Express*, June 19 1941.

2ND NARRATOR: 'A number of French prisoners of war returned and were welcomed by the Mayor of Lyons on behalf of Marshal Pétain.' (*Sings 'Maréchal Nous Voilà', the song of the Pétainists.*)
Maréchal, nous voilà!
Devant toi, le sauveur de la France,
Nour jurons, nous tes gars,
Des servir et de suivre tes pas
Maréchal, nous voilà!
Tu nous a redonné l'espérance
La patrie renaîtra
Maréchal, Maréchal nous voilà!

1ˢᵀ NURSE: Mr Roosevelt's dilemma.

2ᴺᴰ NARRATOR: Whether to join the European War

1ˢᵀ NARRATOR: ...or not.

GESTAPO OFFICER: 'A trade and clearing agreement has been concluded at Agram between Hungary and Croatia.'

2ᴺᴰ NARRATOR: 'The British mail steamer St Patrick of 2,000 tons engaged on the service between England and Ireland

1ˢᵀ NARRATOR: ...was sunk as a result of an attack by a German plane on June 13 1941.'

GESTAPO OFFICER: 'Great success in assuring the nation's food supplies has been achieved in Germany.'

1ˢᵀ NARRATOR: 'While cycling down *Les Baisseries* last evening, Miss A. Falla, an employee of the telephone exchange, came into contact with another cycle ridden by Miss Amy of Monument Gardens. As a result Miss Falla is suffering from a dislocated shoulder.'

GESTAPO OFFICER: 'Blackout Dusk to Dawn.'

2ᴺᴰ NARRATOR: '*Couvrefeu* – Curfew.'

GESTAPO OFFICER: 'Nine p.m. to 6 a.m.'.

1ˢᵀ NARRATOR: *La Gazette Officielle.* (*Gives everyone a newspaper.*)

1ˢᵀ NURSE: The *Evening Press.*

1ˢᵀ NARRATOR: 'Second Order relating to Measures Against Jews.'

GESTAPO OFFICER: '*Zweite Verordnung über Massnahmen gegen Juden.*'

2ᴺᴰ NARRATOR: 'All Jewish economic enterprises, or any enterprises which have been Jewish since May 23 1940, are to be declared by October 31 1940 to the competent local authorities.'

GESTAPO OFFICER: *Jüdische wirtschaftliche Unternehmen oder solche wirtschaftlichen Unternehmen, die nach dem 23 Mai 1940 noch jüdisch gewesen sind, sind bis zum 31 Oktober 1940 bei dem zustandigen Unterpraefekten anzumelden.*'
Jews cannot take part in

SCULPHER: 'Wholesale and retail trade.'

GESTAPO OFFICER: 'Hotel and catering industry.'

SCULPHER: 'Navigation.'

GESTAPO OFFICER: 'Banking and money exchange.'

1ST NARRATOR: 'Dealing in automatic machines.'

GESTAPO OFFICER: 'Third Order.'

SCULPHER: 'Relating to Measures Against Jews April 26 1941.'

GESTAPO OFFICER: 'Jews.'

1ST NURSE: 'Any person having at least three grandparents of pure Jewish blood.'

2ND NARRATOR: 'A Jewish grandparent,

SCULPHER: ...a person married to a Jew,

1ST NURSE: ...or who subsequently marries a Jew

THERESA: ...shall be deemed to be a Jew.'

SCULPHER: 'In doubtful cases

1ST NURSE: ...a person shall be deemed to be a Jew.'

1ST NARRATOR: 'We are informed by Essential Commodities that there will be half a ration of meat issued this weekend.'

1ST NURSE: 'Beef or veal.'

2ND NARRATOR: 'F. Beckford Funeral Undertaker. Motor hearse and cars supplied. The trade supplied.'

1ST NURSE: 'St George's Hall open for Roller Skating every Tuesday, Thursday and Saturday 7 till 10 p.m.'.

1ST NARRATOR: 'Gaumont Cinema this week. *Ein Leben Lang.*'

1ST NURSE: Her whole life.

2ND NARRATOR: Fascinating German film.

THERESA: English subtitles.

GESTAPO OFFICER: 'Jews are forbidden to go to the cinema, cafés.'

THERESA: They talk of slave workers here on Guernsey.

1ST NARRATOR: I see them all. The Spanish Republican digging with his hands into the sides of the hill, digging to make the military hospital.

GESTAPO OFFICER: Operation Todt.

2ND NARRATOR: Operation Death.

1ST NARRATOR: They beat and beat him till he hit back. They didn't kill him.

GESTAPO OFFICER: This time.

1ˢᵀ NURSE: The Jews? Where are they? They just seemed to disappear...

2ᴺᴰ NARRATOR: The Germans didn't weed out the Jews.

THERESA: They didn't need to.

SCULPHER: List of Jews resident in Guernsey.

GESTAPO OFFICER: One: Dumequin.

1ˢᵀ WOMAN: (*As character.*) *Née* Fink.

SCULPHER: Religion?

1ˢᵀ WOMAN: (*As character.*) Church of England.

GESTAPO OFFICER: Two: Brouard.

2ᴺᴰ WOMAN: (*As character.*) *Née* Bauer.

SCULPHER: Three: Spitz.

SPITZ: Auguste. Born Vienna.

SCULPHER: Occupation?

SPITZ: Domestic.

SCULPHER: Religion?

SPITZ: Jewish.

SCULPHER: Four: Steiner. Theresa.

1ˢᵀ NURSE: Yes. Theresa Steiner, that's her.

SCULPHER: Born?

THERESA: Vienna.

SCULPHER: Occupation?

THERESA: Nurse.

SCULPHER: Religion?

THERESA: Jewish.

GESTAPO OFFICER: *Jude.*

CASSANDRA: *Pauvre juive.*

SCULPHER: From the Island Police to the Gestapo.
Sir. I have the *honour to report* that the Jews resident in the Bailiwick of Guernsey are of the following nationalities: British: Dumequin, Elizabeth (*née* Fink); British: Brouard, Elda (*née* Bauer), 109 Victoria Road; German: Steiner, Theresa, Castel Hospital; German: Spitz, Auguste, Castel Hospital; Czech: Wranowsky, Annie, Clos de Ville, Sark. I have the honour to be, sir, Your Obedient Servant.

2ᴺᴰ NARRATOR: I have the honour to be

THERESA: ...sir

SCULPHER: ...your obedient servant.

THERESA: Guernsey Police Inspector.

1ST NARRATOR: W. R. Schulpher.

2ND NARRATOR: Letter from A. J. Roussel Esq, His Majesty's Greffier, Royal Court, Guernsey.

1ST NARRATOR: Dear Sir.

THERESA: Re: Relating to Measures Against Jews.

2ND NARRATOR: I have to report that this office has taken charge of the stock of a small wholesale ladies underclothing business which was abandoned at the time of the evacuation.

2ND NARRATOR: I understand it was conducted by a

1ST NARRATOR: ...Mrs W. Middlewick at her private residence at 36 High Street

2ND NARRATOR: ...who I believe was of the Jewish faith. The business has not been carried on since the stock was taken over.

1ST NARRATOR: The stock consists of

2ND NARRATOR: ...143 pairs of ladies artificial silk stockings;

1ST NARRATOR: ...186 ladies vests;

2ND NARRATOR: ...992 pairs of knickers;

1ST NARRATOR: ...20 combinations;

2ND NARRATOR: ...378 slips;

1ST NARRATOR: ...four coats summer weight;

2ND NARRATOR: ...12 coats winter weight;

1ST NARRATOR: ...six costumes;

2ND NARRATOR: ...nine cotton frocks;

1ST NARRATOR: ...five wool frocks;

2ND NARRATOR: ...64 nightdresses;

1ST NARRATOR: ...21 suits pyjamas.

SCULPHER: Letter to the Gestapo. Sir.

1ST WOMAN: (*As character.*) Julia Brichta.

2ND WOMAN: (*As character.*) Hungarian.

SCULPHER: I beg to report that I have seen the above-named woman. As far as she is concerned –

1ST WOMAN: (*As character.*) My parents aren't Jews. I'm not a Jew. (*Crosses herself frantically.*)

2ND WOMAN: (*As character.*) Annie Wranowsky.

1ST NARRATOR: German.

SCULPHER: Enquiries have been made by the Senechal of Sark within the Bailiwick of Guernsey concerning the above-named woman.

2ND WOMAN: (*As character.*) Neither my parents nor my grandparents were Jews.

SCULPHER: Her passport, number 558 issued in London

2ND NARRATOR: ...on the thirteenth of February 1939,

SCULPHER: ...is stamped with a J.

1ST NARRATOR: I am your

SCULPHER: ...obedient servant.

1ST NARRATOR: W. R. Schulpher.

2ND NARRATOR: Inspector, Guernsey.

THERESA: Letter to the Gestapo.

1ST NARRATOR: Dear Sir, I have the honour to be your obedient servant.

THERESA: Order Relating to Measures Against the Jews.

2ND NARRATOR: Regarding the registration of Jews.

1ST NARRATOR: I have the honour to report that the Order

2ND NARRATOR: ...which accompanied your letter

1ST NARRATOR: ...was communicated

2ND NARRATOR: ...to the Royal Court of Guernsey.

1ST NARRATOR: I can assure you that there will be no delay in so far as I am concerned in furnishing you with the information you require. I have the honour to be

2ND NARRATOR: ...your obedient servant.

1ST NARRATOR: ...your obedient servant.

THERESA: Signed

1ST NARRATOR: ...Victor G. Carey. Bailiff.

(*Blackout.*)

Josef's Letter

JOSEF has a blank sheet of paper in his hand.

JOSEF: Dear Mother
I write this because I know you'll never receive it. I made a mistake not coming with you. Now I'll never be an English butler.

Strange to think this is my last day of life. It's brave to take your own life, don't you think? Better that it happens this way.

I saw the Nazis beating an old Jew and dragging him into the public lavatory in the Opera House. They made him clean the lavatory with his bare hands. Then they made him smear the shit on his face. After they'd finished laughing they crushed his head on the ground until the blood spilt all over the marble floor. Why did I watch? Why didn't I stop them? And if I'd tried, my head would now be crushed. They are taking us to Dachau. So far I've escaped but time runs short. I don't want to go to Dachau. They'd send you a parcel of my ashes and ask you to pay the postage. It's better this way. Better to be a Stoic in the old Roman fashion, don't you think, Mother?

Many of my old schoolfriends have disappeared. Vicki, my first girlfriend. Do you remember her, Mother? You were quite jealous. Vicki went to Dachau. (*Sings phrases from 'The Blue Danube' and speaks at the same time; the effect is of a vocal struggle as his singing voice fights with his speaking voice.*) They shoot Jews on the banks of the River Danube and in the ballrooms people still waltz. Vienna still looks the same. The opera houses and cafés are still full. And when we disappear nobody notices.

They say the war will mean a Third Reich that lasts for a thousand years. *Reich* means rich. The National Socialists are interested in money. And you in London, Mother, maybe it'll work out better for you. Are you a maid to some rich English lady? They say the English are good people, good to foreigners and that they don't hate the Jews too much. But, when the Nazis get to England, where will you hide?

There's so much I haven't done, so much I haven't seen, Mother. Nobody will ever know my name. Nobody will ever remember me. Only you. In the last moments before I die I will think of you.

(*Wryly.*)Don't worry. I've already forgotten Vicki.

(*Crushes paper defiantly.*)

The Guernsey Girl

Crossfade to St Peter's Port, Guernsey.

GERMAN SOLDIER: Your bike, Fräulein, is there something wrong?

GIRL: Yes. The tyre's gone.

GERMAN SOLDIER: May I help you?

GIRL: I don't know.

GERMAN SOLDIER: Does your father have a car?

GIRL: He did have. Before...the Germans took it.

GERMAN SOLDIER: Where do you live?

GIRL: Not far. Street number 15.

GERMAN SOLDIER: What was the name of the street before?

GIRL: Before?

GERMAN SOLDIER: Before we came?

GIRL: Margaret Street.

GERMAN SOLDIER: And now the names are all changed to numbers.

GIRL: I think I prefer that.

GERMAN SOLDIER: Do you?

GIRL: Where are you from?

GERMAN SOLDIER: München.

GIRL: München. Where is that?

GERMAN SOLDIER: In the south of Germany.

GIRL: München.

GERMAN SOLDIER: Have you been to Germany?

GIRL: I've never been out of Guernsey. Except for a day trip to Jersey. But we don't like Jersey people.

GERMAN SOLDIER: You'd like Germany.

GIRL: Why?

GERMAN SOLDIER: There's more fun there than here. In camp we call this the arsehole of the world. Oh excuse me.

GIRL: Why do you call it that?

GERMAN SOLDIER: It's so dull here. We have theatres, cafés, opera. There's nothing to do here. But wait.

GIRL: Wait for what?

GERMAN SOLDIER: For the war to end.

GIRL: And you'll win?

GERMAN SOLDIER: *Heute Frankreich. Morgen England.* Today France. Tomorrow England.

GIRL: You're right. It is dull here. The blackout. The curfew.

GERMAN SOLDIER: There is the cinema.

GIRL: German films.

GERMAN SOLDIER: With subtitles.

GIRL: Yes.

GERMAN SOLDIER: I'd love to take you but we can't sit with you. (*Pause.*) You're very pretty.

GIRL: Am I?

GERMAN SOLDIER: Yes. Very pretty.

GIRL: You speak English well. Where did you learn?

GERMAN SOLDIER: In school. I like Shakespeare. *Julius Caesar.* 'The fault, dear Brutus, is not in our stars, but in ourselves, that we are underlings.'

GIRL: I don't know any quotations.

GERMAN SOLDIER: I could bring you some coffee. Do you like coffee? Or new clothes? A silk blouse, perhaps? They sell them in our shops. They are brought over from Paris. For the officers to buy for their wives. I'll get you one if you'll see me again. Tomorrow?

GIRL: A silk blouse. Yes, I'd like that.

GERMAN SOLDIER: Tomorrow then. Same time. Here on road 19.

GIRL: I'll be here.

GERMAN SOLDIER: Heil Hitler.

GIRL: Heil Hitler.

(*Hold the GIRL in spot. She's giving the Hitler salute. The same actress plays the role of the 1ST NURSE in the next scene which suggests she's the same character. The Radetsky March links the scenes.*)

Castel Hospital Guernsey

Three NURSES (SPITZ, THERESA and 1ST NURSE) shaking sheets to the Radetsky March. SCULPHER looks on. The scene opens in mid-conversation.

1ST NURSE: No no no, he's not a doctor.

SPITZ: Really?

THERESA: A doctor can be a doctor without being a medical doctor you know.

1ST NURSE: (*To audience.*) They know everything, these 'continentals'.

THERESA: (*Beckons SPITZ.*) Vienna?
(*SPITZ nods.*)
I remember you. One day in the park. I was walking with my son. I saw you on the bench. The bench where Jews were forbidden to sit.

SCULPHER: No Jews

GESTAPO OFFICER: ...are allowed

THERESA: ...to sit.

SPITZ: To sit.

THERESA: I heard you were a Communist.

SCULPHER: A Jew *and* a Communist.

THERESA: Your father repaired shoes.
Spitz?

SPITZ: Auguste. From Vienna.

SCULPHER: Spitz.

THERESA: I heard someone say there's another woman on the island.

SCULPHER: Another Jewess on the island. Theresa Steiner AND Auguste Spitz AND

NURSE: ...Marianne Grünfeld from Silesia.
(*Light change.*
GESTAPO OFFICER clicks his fingers. SCULPHER stands behind him. Both are in spotlight.)

GESTAPO OFFICER: The Guernsey Police have been most helpful. In fact the island authorities – although they consider themselves British – have behaved like true servants of the Reich. We shall certainly have no trouble here. If the British are going to be so helpful then there's no need to worry about any trouble once we take the mainland.

I don't know why we are at war with England at all. As you can see a spirit of co-operation and willingness to help us root out these Jews means we can quickly clean up the island.

These three women can be shipped to Auschwitz as soon as we are ready for the transport.

Order to Paris. Three Yellow Stars. *Sofort!*

Theresa's Dormitory

Blackout. GESTAPO OFFICER with torch.

GESTAPO OFFICER: Where is she? Where's Theresa Steiner? You, Matron, you're in charge, tell me where she is.

MATRON: Of course, Herr Kommandant. Theresa Steiner is one of my nurses. She's upstairs in the nurses' dormitory. Nurse Oldman will take you.

(*He shines torch on 1ST NURSE who points to THERESA sleeping.*)

GESTAPO OFFICER: Theresa Steiner. You have three minutes to pack one suitcase before you leave with me.

THERESA: Leave with you? Why? What's happening?

GESTAPO OFFICER: All Jews are being taken off the island.

THERESA: Why?

GESTAPO OFFICER: Pack immediately. Unless you want the rest of the nurses to suffer.

(*NURSES throw case, coat and hat at THERESA.*
Final image of GESTAPO OFFICER standing behind THERESA. Hold in spot. Bring up sound of trains. Mix with 'The Blue Danube' echo. Return to high volume trains going to Auschwitz and slow blackout.)

The End.

A DEAD WOMAN ON HOLIDAY

Dedicated to Alain Carpentier

Characters

TWO STAND-UP COMEDIANS

SOPHIA GOLDENBERG
a French Jew

PAUL CARVER
a GI during the war, now interpreter at the Trials

DEE DEE CARVER
Paul's wife, in her thirties

VINCENT WILDING
husband of Sophia, former soldier in British Army

GERMAN WOMAN
a former concentration camp guard, in her thirties

FOREIGN OFFICE BUREAUCRAT

AMERICAN JUDGE

WAITER

INTERPRETER

A Dead Woman on Holiday was first produced at the Holborn Centre for Performing Arts on 14 October 1991, with the following cast:

TWO STAND-UP COMEDIANS, Martin Boileau,
    Kate Morgan

SOPHIA GOLDENBERG, Monique Burg

PAUL CARVER, Nick Miles

DEE DEE CARVER, Kate Margam

VINCENT WILDING, Martin Boileau

GERMAN WOMAN, Bettina von Knebel

FOREIGN OFFICE BUREAUCRAT, Nick Miles

Director, Julia Pascal

Lighting Design, Ian Watts

Sound design, Colin Brown

Notes:

The production can be performed by six or more actors.

The action takes place in London and Nuremberg between 1945 and 1946.

The play runs two hours without an interval.

Acknowledgements:

Thanks to the Imperial War Museum for access to archive film on the Nuremberg Trials. Thanks also to Thomas Kampe for the German translations, Alain Carpentier for the French translations and Goar Laupus for the Russian translations.

Prologue

*Two STAND-UP COMEDIANS, one male and one female, serve as
satirical travel guides in Germany. They will be known only as ONE
and TWO. They play in vaudeville or German cabaret style.*

Lights up.

ONE: And welcome to your holiday in Germany. Don't
    forget that the most important thing is to enjoy yourself!

TWO: Aren't you the lucky ones! Not only are you going to
    Germany but you're going to the south of Germany.

ONE: Whatever you do, don't forget your Baedeker Travel
    Guide of 1936.

TWO: Nuremberg, that golden city of Albrecht Dürer and
    the Master Singers, boasts one of the most amazing
    stadiums in the whole world.

ONE: The Party Rally Grounds

TWO: ...(or *Das Reichsparteitag Gelände*)

ONE: ...is a huge area laid out for mass demonstrations and
    march pasts

TWO: ...of the National Socialist Party's Rally which has
    taken place here every year since 1933.

ONE: In this stadium you can stand 120,000 men and don't
    forget to go and see the grandstand which is flanked
    with 23-foot-high golden eagles.

TWO: There is also a large lake with open air restaurants,

ONE: ...rowing boats, a café and a swimming pool.

TWO: The best hotel in Nuremberg

ONE: ...is the Grand Hotel with nearly five hundred beds.

TWO: A double bed in Germany is called

ONE: ...*ein Französisches Bett,*

TWO: ...a French bed.

ONE: When you change your money from pounds sterling

TWO: ...don't forget that the German currency is

ONE: ...the *Reichsmark.*

TWO: Useful vocabulary for the traveller.

ONE: *Friedhof*:

TWO: ...cemetery;

ONE: *Kirche*:

TWO: ...church;

ONE: *unter*:

TWO: ...lower;

ONE: *Mensch*:

TWO: ...man;

ONE: *der Tank*:

TWO: ...tank;

ONE: *der Wagenführer*:

TWO: ...driver.

ONE: The train service is the best in Europe.

TWO: There are many frequent trains from

ONE: ...France,

TWO: ...Czechoslovakia,

ONE: ...Poland,

TWO: ...Holland,

ONE: ...Belgium,

TWO: ...Luxembourg,

ONE: ...Greece,

TWO: ...Yugoslavia,

ONE: ...Croatia

TWO: ...and Serbia,

ONE: ...Hungary,

TWO: ...Romania.

ONE: Watch out for those colourful gypsies in these countries:

TWO: ...Lithuania,

ONE: ...Italy,

TWO: ...most of Soviet Russia

ONE: ...and even the Channel Islands.

TWO: Foreigners spending at least seven days in Germany are granted a reduction of 60% on the German Railways.

ONE: Language.

TWO: Tourists who do not deviate from the beaten track will find that English is understood at the principal hotels and the usual resorts of strangers

ONE: ...but the traveller's previous study of German will be amply repaid in the course of his journey.

TWO: More useful vocabulary.

ONE: *Kreuz*:

TWO: ...cross;

ONE: *Flughafen*:

TWO: ...airport;

ONE: *Eisenbahn*:

TWO: ...railway;

ONE: *Ausgang*:

TWO: ...exit.

ONE: Public Holiday:

TWO: ...April 20,

ONE: ...Hitler's birthday.

TWO: September – the beginning.

ONE: National Socialist Party Rally in Nuremberg.

TWO: Outline of German history.

ONE: Among the population of the Nordic cultural sphere, the

TWO: ...Germans began to be recognisable in the Bronze Age (1800 BC).

ONE: Nuremberg is a town of 400,000 inhabitants and lies in a sandy plain partly clothed with fir trees.

TWO: Nuremberg is a commercial city and manufacturing town in southern Germany.

It produces metalware, lead pencils, machinery, toys

ONE: ...and gingerbread.

TWO: Nearby Munich houses the National Theatre in the Residenz; here there is a small auditorium of rare charm and rococo decoration.

ONE: Close to this is the memorial to the 16 National Socialists who fell in the fighting of 1933.

TWO: Passersby to salute with the *Deutsche Grüss*,

ONE: ...right arm extended accompanied by the words

TWO: ...'Heil Hitler'.

ONE: This has largely superseded the practice of hat-raising.

TWO: The National Socialist Party, the sole party of the Reich, has its headquarters at Munich.

ONE: The leader of the party is Adolf Hitler, his deputy is Rudolf Hess.

TWO: Perhaps the most comfortable way of reaching Germany from England is by a transatlantic liner from Southampton

ONE: ...or Plymouth to Hamburg or Bremen

TWO: ...or there are daily air services from Croydon.

ONE: While you are in Munich don't forget to go to the Alte Pinakothek, one of the oldest galleries in Europe, where an English version of the catalogue is on sale.

TWO: There you will see work by the great Flemish artist, Rubens. You can see his

ONE: ...'Massacre of the Innocents',

TWO: ...'The Last Judgement',

ONE: ...and 'The Fall of the Damned'.

ONE: You can travel from Nuremberg to Munich express via Augsburg or Donauworth.

TWO: In Donauworth you will see the fourteenth-century tombstone of Mary of Brabant who was beheaded in 1256 by order of her husband,

ONE: ...Duke Ludwig the Severe,

TWO: ...or go to Essen. Yes, go to Alfred Krupps' factories for a tour of the machinery, locomotives and industrial engineering.

ONE: The welfare arrangements instituted by Krupps for his workers are unsurpassed.

TWO: In the hotels no tips should be given

ONE: ...except perhaps to the porter if he has rendered any special services.

TWO: Trains.

ONE: There are three classes with compartments for smokers,

TWO: ...non-smokers

ONE: ...and ladies.

TWO: National emblems.

ONE: The swastika

TWO: ...(*Hakenkreuz* or hooked cross) now has its place on every

ONE: ...national emblem.

TWO: National anthem.

ONE: *Deutschland Über Alles*.

TWO: What year did you say this Baedeker was?

ONE: It's 1936.

TWO: But we're in 1945 now.

ONE: Mr Carl Baedeker does not seem to have found time
for a reprint.

TWO: More useful vocabulary.

ONE: *Arbeit*:

TWO: ...work.

ONE: Work?

TWO: No thanks, I'd rather stay at home.

(*Blackout.*)

London 1945

SOPHIA in a spotlight. She is being interviewed by an ENGLISH
FOREIGN OFFICE BUREACRAT. Mozart's Mass in C Minor
KV427.

BUREAUCRAT: This work, do you realise what it entails?

SOPHIA: Translating into English or French. Translating
from German.

BUREAUCRAT: No problems about your ability. You have
studied English, German — and of course no need to
discuss the French. You studied at the Sorbonne in
Paris.

SOPHIA: Yes.

BUREAUCRAT: Before the war?

SOPHIA: Before the war.

BUREAUCRAT: And your thesis was interrupted by the
invasion of the Nazis?

SOPHIA: Yes.

BUREAUCRAT: Between 1941 and 1945 you worked for
our Intelligence?

SOPHIA: That's correct.

BUREAUCRAT: Just as a matter of curiosity, what was the
title of your thesis?

SOPHIA: 'Against Romantic Love: A Discourse on the
Princess of Cleves by Madame de Lafayette.'

BUREAUCRAT: You are a very attractive woman, if you
don't mind me saying so, and you want me to
understand that you don't believe in love?

SOPHIA: After Auschwitz — do you?

BUREAUCRAT: It's your thesis, Miss Goldenberg. Not mine. And I believe that you started it before the war.

SOPHIA: Of course I believe in love, it's the idea of falling in love which I question.

BUREAUCRAT: Quite.

Now, let's get back to your history. You were born in 1913 in Alsace. Your parents were German immigrants to France. Your father was a doctor, your mother a tailoress. You were the late child of elderly parents. They died naturally.

SOPHIA: No. They committed suicide in 1940.

BUREAUCRAT: My mistake. They committed suicide in 1940. How exactly did they do that, Miss Goldenberg?

SOPHIA: With a revolver.

BUREAUCRAT: I see.

SOPHIA: I came to England in 1940 as the Nazis invaded Paris.

BUREAUCRAT: You got married.

SOPHIA: Yes. I am Mrs Vincent Wilding.

BUREAUCRAT: Your husband?

SOPHIA: Is a corporal in the British Army. He fought in France. Dunkirk.

BUREAUCRAT: I've examined his records. A fine soldier.

SOPHIA: Yes, a fine soldier.

BUREAUCRAT: You married beneath yourself.

SOPHIA: Did I?

BUREAUCRAT: Class is of importance.

SOPHIA: I know.

BUREAUCRAT: Uneducated, working class.

SOPHIA: But 'a fine soldier'.

BUREAUCRAT: You're bourgeois, intellectual, liberal. How do you put up with it?

SOPHIA: With what?

BUREAUCRAT: The class difference.

SOPHIA: There is always love.

BUREAUCRAT: But you don't believe in love.

SOPHIA: That's not what I said.

BUREAUCRAT: Excuse me. I'm not here to discuss your marriage. It's just that I'm a curious man, Mrs Wilding.

SOPHIA: I prefer my maiden name.

BUREAUCRAT: And why is that, Miss Goldenberg? Anonymity? Or do you like to be seen as – shall we say – an 'unattached woman'? The word 'spinster' seems rather inappropriate in your case.

SOPHIA: No, none of those reasons. It's just that I prefer to be known as a Jew.

(*Blackout.*

Crossfade to Nuremberg Trials.)

Nuremberg 1945. The Courthouse

The scene starts with SOPHIA interpreting and then the other INTERPRETERS take over. The text can either be performed in English with lines assigned to various INTERPRETERS to give the impression of multiple and simultaneous translations or it can be delivered in English with either French, German or Russian overlapping. Translations in all three languages follow this speech.

INTERPRETER: October fifth 1943 at Dubno in the Ukraine.

SOPHIA: The people who had got off the trucks – men, women and children of all ages – had to undress on the orders of an SS man. All these people had the regulation yellow patches on their clothes and could be recognised as Jews. I saw a heap of shoes, about eight hundred to a thousand pairs, great piles of underlinen and clothing. Without screaming or weeping these people undressed and stood around in family groups, kissing each other, and saying farewell. During the fifteen minutes that I stood near I heard no complaints or plea for mercy. I watched a family of about eight persons, a man and a woman both about fifty with some children of about one, eight and ten, and two grown-up daughters of about twenty and twenty-four. An old woman with snow white hair was holding the one-year-old child in her arms and singing to it and tickling it. The child was cooing in delight. The couple were looking on with tears in their eyes. The father was holding the hand of a boy about ten years old and speaking to him softly. The boy was fighting his tears. The father pointed to the sky, stroked his head and seemed to explain something to him. At that moment the SS man at the pit shouted something to his comrade. The latter counted off about twenty persons and instructed them to go behind the earth mound. Among them was this family. I well remember a girl, slim with black hair who, as she passed close to me, pointed to herself and said "Twenty-three". I walked round the mound and found myself confronted by a tremendous grave. People were closely wedged together and lying on top of each other so that only their heads were visible. Nearly all had blood running over their shoulders from their heads. Some of the people shot were still moving. Some were lifting their arms and turning their heads to show that they were still alive. The pit was already two thirds full. I estimated that it already contained about a thousand people. I looked for the man who did the shooting. He was an SS man who sat at the edge of the pit. He had a tommy gun on his knee and was smoking a cigarette. The people, completely naked, went down some steps which were cut in the clay wall of the pit and clambered over the heads of the people lying there, to the place which the SS man directed them. They lay down in front of the dead or injured people; some caressed those who were still alive and spoke to them in a low voice. Then I heard a series of shots. I looked into the pit and saw that the bodies were twitching. Blood was running from their necks. I was surprised that I was not ordered away. The next batch was approaching. They went down into the pit, lined themselves up against the previous victims and were shot. When I walked back around the mound I noticed another truckload of people which had just arrived. This time it included sick and infirm persons. An old, very thin woman, with terribly thin legs, was undressed by others who were already naked, while two people held her up. The woman appeared to be paralysed. The

naked people carried the woman around to the mound.
I left with my foreman and drove in my car back to
Dubno. (*SOPHIA vomits.*)

FRENCH INTERPRETER: *Les gens qui étaient descendus des
camions – hommes, femmes et enfants de tous âges – devaient
se deshabillér par ordre du SS. Tous ces gens portaient l'étoile
jaune réglementaire sur leurs vêtements en tant que juifs. Je vis
un tas de chaussures, environ huit cents à milles paires, de
grandes piles de sous vêtements et de vêtements. Sans crier ni
pleurer ces gens se rassemblaient par familles, s'embrassant et se
disant adieu. Durant les quinze minutes que je passais là je
n'entendis ni plaintes ni appel à la pitié. J'observais une famille
d'environ huit personnes, un homme et une femme d'à peu près
cinquante ans avec quelques enfants d'environ un, huit et
dix ans et deux grandes filles d'environ vingt ans. Une vieille
femme aux cheveux blancs avait pris le jeune enfant de un an
dans ses bras et chantait en le berçant. L'enfant gazouillait de
plaisir. Le couple les regardait les larmes aux yeux. Le père avait
pris la main d'un garçon de dix ans et lui parlait doucement.
Le garçon luttait contre ses larmes. Le père, montrant le ciel, lui
tapotait la tête et semblait lui expliquer quelquechose. A cet
instant le SS près de l'excavation creusée dans la terre cria
quelque chose à son camarade. Ce dernier compta environ vingt
personnes et leur ordonna d'aller se placer derrière le monticule de
terre. Parmi eux il y avait cette famille. Je me souviens très bien
d'une fille, maigre avec des cheveux noirs qui, alors qu'elle
passait près de moi, pointait son index sur la poitrine en
disant, "Vingt trois." Je contournais le monticule et me
retrouvais face à une fosse énorme. Les gens étaient étroitement
entrêmelés et allongés les uns sur les autres ce qui fait que seules
leurs têtes étaient visibles. Presque tout avait du sang qui leur
coulait de la tête sur les épaules. Certains de ces suppliciés
bougaient encore. Quelques uns levaient les bras et tournaient la
tête pour montrer qu'ils étaient encore en vie. L'excavation était
déjà remplie aux deux tiers. J'estimais qu'elle devait contenir
presque cent personnes. Je cherchais l'homme qui déclenchait la
fusillade. C'était un SS qui était assis au bord du trou. Il avait
une mitraillette sur le genous et fumait une cigarette. Les gens,
completement nus descendaient quelque marches taillées dans*

l'argile et grimpaient sur les têtes de ceux qui étaient étendus jusqu'à la place que leur indiquait le SS. Ils se tenaient face aux mortes ou aux blessés quelques un carassaient ceux qui étaient encore en vie et leur parlaient à voix basse. Alors j'entendis une série de détonations. Je regardais dans le trou et je vis que les corps se contractaient nerveusement. Du sang coulait de leurs cous. J'étais surpris de ne pas avoir reçu l'ordre de partir. La prochaine fournée approchait. Ils descendaient dans le trou, s'alignant commes les précédents et furent exécutés. En contournant à nouveau le monticule je remarquais qu'un autre chargement de gens venait juste d'arriver. Cette fois il comportait des malades et des infirmes. Une vielle femme très maigre avec des jambes horriblement minces fut deshabillée par les autres qui étaient déjà nus tandis que deux personnes la soutenaient. Cette femme semblait paralysée. Les gens nus transporterent cette femme derrière le monticule. Je rejoignis mon contremaître et reparti en voiture jusqu'à Dubno.

GERMAN INTERPRETER: *Die Menschen, die aus den Lastwagen kamen, Männer, Frauen und Kinder jeden Alters, mussten sich auf Befehl der SS Männer entkleiden. All diese Menschen hatten Gelbe Sterne auf Ihrer Kleidung und waren leicht als Juden zu erkennen. Ich sah einen Haufen Schuhe, etwa zwischen Achthundert und Eintausend Paare, grosse Haufen von Unterwäsche und Bekleidung. Diese Menschen entkleideten sich ohne zu weinen oder zu schreien und standen in Familiengruppen zusammen, sich küssend und sich verabschiedend. Waehrend der fünfzehn Minuten, die ich dort verbrachte, hörte ich keine Beschwerden oder Rufe nach Erlösung. Ich beobachtete eine Familie von acht Personen, ein Mann und eine Frau von ungefähr fünfzig Jahren mit mehreren Kindern im Alter von ein, acht und zehn Jahren, und zwei erwachsenen Töchtern von ungefähr zwanzig und vierundzwanzig Jahren. Eine alte Frau mit schneeweissem Haar hielt ein einjähriges Kind, sang zu ihm und kitzelte es. Das Kind lachte vor Vergnügen. Das Paar schaute sich mit Tränen in den Augen an. Der Vater hielt die Hand eines ungefähr zehn jährigen Jungen und flüsterte sanft zu ihm. Der Junge kämpfte mit seinen Tränen. Der Vater zeigte zum Himmel, streichelte den Kopf des Jungen und schien Ihm irgendetwas zu* *erklären. Dann schrie der SS Mann an der Grube irgendetwas zu seinem Kameraden. Dieser teilte zwanzig Menschen von der Gruppe und orderte sie hinter den Erdhügel zu laufen. In der Gruppe war auch diese Familie. Ich kann mich gut an ein Madchen aus dieser Gruppe erinnern. Sie zeigte mit dem Finger auf sich selbst und   sagte dann, "Dreiundzwanzig." Ich ging um den Erdhaufen herum und sah plötzlich ein riesiges Grab. Die Menschen waren eng aneinander gedrückt, und lagen aufeinander, so dass man nur noch ihre Köpfe sah. Fast allen lief Blut vom Kopf uber die Schultern. Manche dieser erschossenen Menschen bewegten sich noch. Einige hoben Ihre Arme und drehten ihre Köpfe um zu zeigen, dass sie noch am Leben waren. Die Grube war fast dreiviertel voll. Ich schätzte, dass dort ungefahr eintausend Menschen lagen. Ich suchte nach dem Mann der die Erschiessungen vornahm. Es war ein SS Mann, der am Ende der Grube sass. Er hatte eine Maschinenpistole ueber seinen Knien und rauchte eine Zigarette. Die völlig nackten Menschen gingen ein paar Stufen herunter, die in die Waende der Grube gegraben waren und kletterten über die Köpfe der Toten bis zu dem Platz der Ihnen von dem SS Mann zugewiesen worden war. Dann legten sie sich vor die Toten oder die Verwundeten. Manche umarmten die Verletzen und flüsterten zu ihnen. Dann hörte ich mehrere Schüsse. Ich schaute in die Grube und sah wie sich die Koerper bewegten und wanden. Aus ihren Nacken rann Blut. Ich wunderte mich, dass man mich nicht wegjagte. Die nächste Gruppe kam. Sie stiegen in die Grube, reihten sich vor den letzen Opfern auf und wurden erschossen. Als ich wieder zuruck hinter den Erdhügel ging sah ich schon die nächste Lastwagenladung von Menschen, die gerade angekommen war. Diesmal waren viele versehrte und kranke Menschen dabei. Eine alte, sehr dünne Frau, mit schrecklich dürren Beinen, wurde von anderen ausgekleidet die auch schon völlig nackt waren, während zwei Menschen sie hochhielten. Die Frau schien gelähmt zu sein. Die Nackten trugen diese Frau hinter den Erdhügel. Dann verliess ich den Platz mit meinem Vorarbeiter und fuhr mit dem Wagen zurück nach Dubno.*

RUSSIAN INTERPRETER: *Lyudi, kotorie soshli s gruzovikov – mujchini, jenschini i deti raznogo vozrasta, doljni bili*

*razdetsya po prikazu esesovzev. U vseh etih lyudey imelis joltie
nashivki na odejde, po kotorim mojno bilo videt, chto oni evrei.
Ya videla gori obuvi, okolo vosmisot ili tisyachi par, ogromnie
stopi belya i odejdi. Bez placha i jalob eti lyudi razdelis i stoyali
razdelivshis po semyam na gruppi, tseluya drug druga i
proschayas. V techenie pyatnadtsati minut, vo vremya kotorih
ya stoyala tam, ya ne slishala jalob ili moleniy o poschade. Ya
videla odnu semyu primerno iz vosmi chelovek, mujchinu i
jenschinu, oba primerno pyatidesyati let, i neskolkih detey okolo
odnogo, vosmi i desyati let i dvuh devushek okolo dvadtsati i
dvadtsati vosmi let. Odna staraya jenschina s belosnejnimi
volosami derjala godovalogo rebyonka na rukah i napevala
yemu, i schekotala yego. Yego golos izdaval vorkuyutschiye
zvuki ot udovolstviya. Roditeli smotreli na eto so slezami na
glazah. Otyets derjal za ruku malchika primerno desyati let i
myagko govoril s nim. Malchik staralsya ne zaplakat. Otyets
ukazal yemu na nyebo i pogladil yego po golovye, kak bi
ob'yasnyaya yemu chto-to. V etot moment esesovets, stoyavshiy
u yami kriknul chto-to cvoyemu naparniku. Tot otschital okolo
dvadtsati chelovek i prikazal im idti za zemlyanuyu nasip.
Sredi teh lyudey bila i eta semya. Ya horosho pomnyu
stroynuyu, temnovolosuyu devushku; kogda ona prohodila
blizko mimo menya, ona ukazala na sebya i skazala:
„Dvadtsat tri." Ya oboshla nasip i okasalas pered gromadnoy
mogiloy. Lyudi bili pritisnuti drug k drugu, lyoja odin na
drugom tak, chto tolko bili vidni ih golovi. Pochti vsyo bilo v
krovi, byeguschey iz golov. Nekotoriye iz pristrelennih eschyo
dvigalis. Nekotoriye iz nih podnimali ruki i povorachivali
golovi, chtobi pokazat, chto oni eschyo jivi. Yama bila uje na
dve treti zapolnena. Ya dumayu, v ney uje bilo okolo tisyachi
chelovek. Ya poiskala glazami togo, kto strelyal. Eto bil
esesovets, kotoriy sidel na krayu yami. On derjal pulemyot na
kolene i kuril sigaretu. Lyudi, razdetiye donaga, soshli vniz po
stupenkam, virezannim v glinyannoy stene yami i karabkalis
po golovam lejavshih tam k mestu, ukazannomu esesovtsem.
Oni legli pered myortvimi ili ranennimi; nekotoriye gladili teh,
kto bil eschyo jiv i tiho zagovarivali s nimi. Potom ya
uslishala seriyu vistrelov. Ya posmotrela v yamu i uvidela, kak
dyorgayutsya tela. Krov tekla iz ih shey. Ya bila udivlena tem,*

chto mne ne prikazali udalitsya. Sleduyuschaya gruppa lyudey priblijalas. Oni soshli v yamu, vistroilis pered prediduschimi jertwami i bili zastreleni. Kogda ya snova oboshla nasip, ya zametila eschyo odin gruzovik, zapolnenniy lyudmi, tolko chto pribivshiy. Na etot raz tam bili bolniye i nemoschniye. Staraya, ochen hudaya jenschina so strashno tonkimi nogami bila razdeta temi, kto uje bil razdet, v to vremya kak dva cheloveka podderjivali yeyo. Eta jenschina bila paralizovana. Nagiye lyudi ponesli jenschinu za nasip. Ya rasstalas s moim nachalnikom i poyehala na svoyey mashine nazad v Dubno. (All freeze and crossfade to spot on GERMAN WOMAN – former concentration camp guard.)

GERMAN WOMAN: But I didn't know anything. How was I to know? We suffered too. My husband was sent away. To France. The French never liked us. They were jealous of our strength. It made them feel inadequate. French men, all fancy talk, no fight. Not like our men. But I suffered – how I suffered. And now, they are always going on and on about the Jews. But that's nothing to what I suffered. The Jews. The Jews. They knew nothing of what I suffered. I lost all my furniture. Half my house destroyed. By the bloody British. Liberators! Huh. They destroyed us. Hitler never disliked the British. After all, they are Aryans too. It's all the Jews' fault. They rule the world. Cosmopolitans. They think they're so clever. Dirty Communists. And the women. Always after our men with their painted faces. Like gypsies. Like the Queen of Sheba they behaved. Whores. And who'll compensate me for my house? My sheets, all burnt. My best linen. An oak table given to me by my grandmother. No one knows how I've suffered. I've no job now. Hitler gave us all employment. But they shut down the camp, those Americans. And Russians, dirty Bolsheviks. They shot at us. I hid. No one could find me. I pretended to be a Jew. You see, I can be as clever as them. Dirty Bolsheviks. I was doing my duty cleaning out those scum. With the gas it was quick. So many women taking away our men with their black eyes and their long hair. Not that we did it, you understand, I wouldn't want to touch a Jew. We did the world a favour. But we didn't finish our job.

We didn't get rid of them all. Some of these soldiers.
I'd swear they are Jews. Russians and Americans. You can
always tell. Even when they hide it with their blond hair
or small noses, there's a hidden Jew there underneath.
It's the hair that gives them away. Fifteen minutes is all it
took. Touch a Jew? Me? Not if I can help it. All that hair.
And then, at Treblinka, we built a fake railway station to
make them believe they were stopping on their way to
resettlement. Resettlement! The only way out of that
place was through the chimney. We sent the Jews to
heaven, we did them a favour. Hitler gave us work,
I earned good money, we ate well, who is going to give
me a wage now? And these Trials. They come to triumph
over us. To humiliate us. These foreigners. Rudolf Hess,
he made the killing easy at Auschwitz. There were six
extermination chambers there. Twenty-four hours a day
we used them. The killing itself was easy. That took the
least time. Once there was a girl who came through alive.
The weight of the bodies trapped an air pocket around
her and she was untouched. What to do with her?
Impossible to let her go after what she'd seen. Who knew
what she would tell. But who would believe her? A crazy
Jew. She was not allowed to live. (*Pause.*)
The killing itself took the least time, it was the burning
of the bodies that took more trouble. No, for the killing
itself you didn't even need guards because the people
went in expecting showers. You could dispose of two
thousand in half an hour. You see it had to be done
otherwise the Jews would have exterminated us.
(*Light change and bring up medieval German music.
SOPHIA has stumbled into a church. PAUL is in shadow
watching SOPHIA.*)

Sophia in a Church

PAUL CARVER enters.

PAUL: Excuse me, I didn't mean to startle you. But I wanted
to talk. I saw you this morning in court. I wanted to ask

you what it's like. Tomorrow is my first day. I don't know if I'll have the courage you have. I don't know why I'm telling you this. (*Pause.*)

Excuse me, perhaps you want to be alone?

SOPHIA: No.

PAUL: Good. (*Pause.*) I'm Paul Carver.

SOPHIA: I'm Sophia Goldenberg.

PAUL: Yes. (*Embarrassed.*)

SOPHIA: You're an American.

PAUL: I guess so.

SOPHIA: From where exactly?

PAUL: Difficult to say. I was born in Pittsburgh. Went to school in Brooklyn, Boston, Milwaukee, Phoenix, Denver, you name it, we lived there.

SOPHIA: Your father was a salesman.

PAUL: How did you know?

SOPHIA: An inspired guess.

PAUL: You're a smart lady. I could see that in court.

SOPHIA: So I'm told.

PAUL: Sorry, I hope you don't think I'm being fresh.

SOPHIA: Being fresh?

PAUL: Well it means, kinda, well kinda. I don't know really. (*Pause.*)

SOPHIA: Do I make you feel uneasy?

PAUL: Hell no. (*Pause.*) Well, maybe just a little.

SOPHIA: Shall we see if we can find a drink somewhere in this ghost town?

(*They leave to go to a bar. A song from the period covers the scene change – can be sung by one of the other actors in cabaret style.*)

Paul and Sophia go to a Bar

PAUL: Hey, this is the only place in the whole of Nuremberg you can get a decent drink and every pressman in the city is here. Americans everywhere. Am I sick to the back teeth of Americans.

(*SOPHIA laughs.*)

Yeah, I guess that's pretty funny coming from me. To you I'm just another American guy, right?

SOPHIA: I wouldn't put it that way.

PAUL: Well, come on, what do you see? I'm just a brash Yank.

SOPHIA: And I'm just a French Jew.

PAUL: You're a Jew. Well, well.

SOPHIA: Don't worry about it.

PAUL: I went to school with Jews, Irish, Italians, Germans. That's what we Yanks are, just a bunch of disguised immigrants.

SOPHIA: Where were your family from?

PAUL: My grandparents say that their grandparents were from Dublin Ireland, Newcastle England and Bremen Germany. So you see I'm a real bastard.

SOPHIA: (*To WAITER.*) Two Scotches.

PAUL: Can I ask you something personal?

SOPHIA: Yes?

PAUL: (*Beat.*) How did you know Scotch is my drink?

SOPHIA: The same way I know you majored in German at Princeton. You have a wife who is waiting at home. And maybe a baby.

PAUL: Two actually. Suzanne and Donald.

SOPHIA: Yes, of course.

PAUL: And you have a husband in France, a country doctor. And no children.

SOPHIA: You're wrong about the country doctor and the husband in France.

PAUL: But there is a husband?

SOPHIA: Yes.

PAUL: That's funny because I was making all that stuff up. You don't even look married.

SOPHIA: Neither do you.

(*Pause.*)

PAUL: You want another drink?

SOPHIA: Yes, why not?

PAUL: I came to Europe for the first time in 1942, you know. They stationed us outside Manchester. Knutsford. This huge mansion was surrounded by

70

grounds. We pitched in those grounds. I used to date some of the girls in Manchester. I never told my wife.

SOPHIA: Why are you telling me?

PAUL: I don't know. Sometimes you can tell a stranger things about yourself that you'd never dare tell anyone else.

SOPHIA: I know.

PAUL: I got married very young. Dee Dee was my first girl. I never even went with a girl before her. Can you believe that?

SOPHIA: Yes.

PAUL: I guess it was to do with those times. My parents told me I had to respect girls, wait until marriage and all that stuff. I guess I thought they were right.

SOPHIA: And now?

PAUL: I don't know. You know, then, I worried about getting a girl pregnant. It was always a great fear. After seeing Dachau I don't know what I feel about anything anymore. I was in France in 1944. I wish I'd seen you then.

SOPHIA: I was in London.

PAUL: I didn't see you there either.

SOPHIA: London's a big place.

PAUL: We shoulda met then, don't you think?

SOPHIA: And my husband?

PAUL: Where was he in 1944?

SOPHIA: Vincent was in France too.

PAUL: Well, I'm glad he wasn't my buddy; especially now I met you.

(*Pause.*)

I was brought up Catholic. I was brought up never to lie. I have to tell you, you make me feel kinda nervous.

SOPHIA: Are you in the Grand Hotel, too?

PAUL: Yeah, well we bombed the hell outa everywhere else and I couldn't find the Y.

SOPHIA: Shall we go to your room?

PAUL: Is that what you want?

SOPHIA: We've both seen a lot of death. Let's not waste any more time. It's what we both want, isn't it?

PAUL: Yes, Sophia, my heart's beating so fast. Since the first moment I saw you my heart beat like a kid of fourteen, can you believe it? (*SOPHIA takes his hand and makes him feel her heart.*)

PAUL: Hey, you're never going to make the next Olympics, not with a heartbeat like that.

News Item / Voice-Over / Scene Link

AMERICAN MALE: And for the first time in history we have a trial in which mass killers stand accused in their own country.
Nuremberg.
There for the first time ordinary men and women have been sought out to do the difficult job of simultaneously translating from one language to another.
The question is *where* to find these talented men and women.
Alfred Steer, administrative head of the Language Division, finds many in the Paris telephone exchange.

A Bedroom in the Grand Hotel

SOPHIA kissing PAUL. He is only wearing underpants. Mozart clarinet concerto.

SOPHIA: Once upon a time, there were three types of human beings on the earth. These humans were doubled. That means they had two heads, four arms, two chests, two stomachs, two sets of genitals, four legs and four feet. There were these three types. One was female, another was male and a third was androgynous. And one day, Zeus decided to cut these human beings in half so that they would have only one head, two arms, one chest, one stomach, one sexual organ, two legs and two feet. So he cut the double female, the double male and the androgynous beings in half so that human beings looked as we look now. But so great was the pain of separation for these humans that they spent all of

their lives searching for the other half. In this way the
females ignored the male part of the world and
searched out their female half; the males ignored
the females and longed for their twin male; and the
androgynous half searched for their twin of the
opposite gender. And all over the world, in every
country, in every town, in every village, there are men
and women searching for their twin soul. They cross
a street and look into the eyes of someone and look for
that spark of knowledge, they look at the back of
someone's head and wonder if it is half their own, they
hear a voice in the street and wonder if the voice is
theirs. It may be another language and partly hidden.
And all over the world there are these beings searching
for their twin souls, their real selves. And there is no
such thing as looking for something or somebody new,
rather they find themselves in the other and when they
find them, they cannot bear to be separated from them,
they yearn for the skin and the touch of the other, they
want to enter into their skin, and with the androgynous
beings the male can penetrate the skin and the body of
the female but she cannot penetrate his and this she
wants to do, she wants to enter into him, to become one
with him as he is with her, she wants to become him
because if she does that then she truly becomes herself.
PAUL: (*As if in orgasm.*) Oh Sophia.

Boogie

*A scene about the learning of translation for the Trials. Different
actors take different lines depending on the emotional ironies. This
should be fairly fast.*

ACTORS: *Homicide involuntaire*:
 ...manslaughter.
Demence:
 ...lunacy.
Aliené:
 ...lunatic.

Misconduct:
...*mavaise conduite.*
Misconduct in a divorce case:
...*inconduite.*
Oath:
...*serment.*
Partner:
...*associé.*
Sleeping partner:
...*associé commanditaire.*
Shoot:
...*tirer;*
...*fusiller.*
Annulment:
...*annulation.*
To annul:
...*annuler;*
...*casser.*
To arrest:
...*arrestation.*
Assassination:
...*assassinat.*
Assault:
...*agression.*
Assault and battery:
...*coups et blessures.*
Indecent assault:
...*attentat à la pudeur.*
Atrocities:
...*atrocités.*
Attachment:
...*saisie-execution.*
Bigamy:
...*bigamie.*
Bribe:
...*concussion;*
...*pot de vin.*
Unbribable:
...*incorruptible.*

Abatement:
... *rabais*.
Abduction:
... *enlevement*.
Abet:
... *encourager*;
... *exciter*;
... *soutenir*.
Abscond:
... *s'enfuir*;
... *déguerpir*;
... *lever le pied*.
Act:
... *acte*;
... *action*;
... *fait*;
... *loi*.
Act of God:
... *cas de force majeur*.
Adultery;
Adulterer;
Adulterous:
... *adultère*;
... *adultère*;
... *adultère*.
Alien:
... *étranger*.
Alimony:
... *pension alimentaire*.
Allegiance:
... *allégeance*;
... *fidelité*.
Annihilation:
... *annihilation*.
Brothel:
... *bordel*;
... *maison de tolerance*;
... *maison close*.

Burial:
...*inhumation*.
Carnal knowledge:
...*rapports sexuels*.
Conspiracy:
...*entente délictueuse*.
Consideration:
...No equivalent in French law.
Marriage contract:
...*contrat de mariage*.
Coroner:
...No equivalent in French law.
Clerk of the Court:
...*greffier*.
Clerical error:
...*erreur de la plume*.
Cohabitation:
...*cohabitation*.
Forced labour (English);
Compulsory labor (American):
...*travaux forcés*.
Concentration camps:
...*camps de concentration*.
Projet de loi:
...a bill.
La note:
...the bill.
Deportation:
...*déportation*.
Wholesale deportation:
...*déportation massive*.
Disorder:
...*désordre*.
Disorderly house:
...*maison mal famée*.
Disorderly conduct:
...*conduite debauchée*.
Divorce:
...*divorce*.

Dowry:
...dot.
Extermination:
...extermination.
Expropriation:
...expropriation.
Mass killings:
...executions collectives.
Liquidation:
...liquidation.
Puppet government:
...gouvernement fantoche.
Death penalty:
...peine de mort.
L'amour:
...love.
La mort:
...death.
(*Blackout.*)

The Trial 2

This starts coolly and then interpretations overlap as the scene gets more and more fractured. Languages intermix as the scene speeds up, provoked by the anger of the investigating committee. The INTERPRETERS can wear headphones. The theatre becomes the Nuremberg courtroom with the audience as part of the process.

PAUL: You'd like to believe that.
How long did it take the German forces to conquer Poland?
How long to drive England off the continent?
How long did it take to overrun Poland, France and take Paris?
FEMALE INTERPRETER: How long did it take to overrun Denmark and Norway?
MALE INTERPRETER: And you want this tribunal to justify you as an officer?
PAUL: You testify that these were all surprises?

SOPHIA: *Vous affirmez que tout cela a été une grande surprise?*
I must ask you to answer the question with a straight yes
or no.

FEMALE INTERPRETER: A straight yes or no is required
here and no explanations.

PAUL: You testify that these were all surprises?

GERMAN INTERPRETER: Did you know that forced
labour was coming from occupied territories to work in
Germany?
*Wüssten Sie dass Zwangsarbeiter aus den Besetzten Gebieten
kamen, um in Deutschland zu arbeiten?*

PAUL: (*Interpreting the GERMAN DEFENDANT's reply.*)
'I only know that the French were forced by their
régime to come.'

SOPHIA: *'Je sais seulement que les français étaient contraints par
leur gouvernement de venir en Allemagne.'*

JUDGE: Are you saying you don't know anything about it?
I want to know what you knew and what you did about it.

SOPHIA: (*Interpreting the GERMAN DEFENDANT's reply.*) *'Je
sais seulement que des gens sont venus volontairement et qu'ils
étaient contents.'*
'I only know that people came voluntarily and that they
were happy.'

RUSSIAN INTERPRETER: (*Interpreting the GERMAN
DEFENDANT's reply.*) *'Ya znayu tolko, chto lyudi prihodili po
sobstvennoy vole i chto oni bili dovolni.'*

PAUL: 'You have spoken of a police state which depended
on the secret police and the concentration camps. Both
the secret police and the concentration camps were
established by Hermann Göring?'
'Answer my question. You can reserve your lectures for
your counsel.'

SOPHIA: *'La police secrète et les camps de concentration 'avaient
été créés, tous les deux, par Hermann Göring.'*

PAUL: 'Answer my question.'

SOPHIA: *'Rèpondez à ma question.'*

PAUL: 'You can save your lectures for your counsel.'

FRENCH INTERPRETER: *'Vous pouvez réserver votre discours
pour votre avocat.'*

ENGLISH INTERPRETER: 'The concentration camps.
Isn't it correct to say that they were established by
Hermann Göring?'

GERMAN DEFENDANT: *Ich weiss nicht.*

JUDGE: Did you do anything to prevent this?

ENGLISH INTERPRETER: (*Female.*) November ninth and
tenth 1938. Did you hear about the decree?

ENGLISH INTERPRETER: (*Male.*) There came a time
when you went to Poland and Soviet Russia did you not?

AMERICAN INTERPRETER: Did you not testify to the
Investigating Committee of the US?

SOPHIA: (*Breaks down – this is not translation.*) I was in
a railway carriage. A young man opposite me was
reading an English newspaper. He began to talk to
me. He was French.
'I am going to Holland,' he told me.
'Why?'
'Because they are nicer to the Jews.'
'Are you a Jew?'
'Yes.'
'Me too.'
An older man sitting opposite me rolled up his sleeve and
showed me his arm. It had a number tatooed on it.
A woman next to him nodded to show that she too was
a Jew.
And there we were. Four Jews. Sitting in a train. Going
to Holland.
Just looking at one another.
And marvelling that we were still alive!

HEAD INTERPRETER: (*American.*) One of my interpreters
is sick. Take her out will you please.
(*Blackout.*)

Sophia's Bedroom in the Grand Hotel

Spotlight on PAUL rocking SOPHIA in his arms.

PAUL: It's okay, honey, it's okay. I got you. I'm holding you.
Sophia, Sophia, I'm here, it's okay.

SOPHIA: When I was a little girl, my father used to carry me. He used to carry me high on his shoulders. Once he took me to the Alps. I was on his back. I was just at the foot of the mountain with him but he teased me and told me we were going to the top. Just my father and me.

PAUL: It's okay, it's okay.

SOPHIA: We didn't go very far but to me it was near heaven. The sun was hot and the air was freezing, both at the same time. It was just like those ice-cream cakes the English make. Do you know what they do, the English?

PAUL: What do they do?

SOPHIA: They take a sponge cake and fill it with ice-cream and then they put it in the oven to cook. And do you know what happens?

PAUL: No.

SOPHIA: The ice cream doesn't melt.

PAUL: Baked Alaska.

SOPHIA: Is that what it's called?

PAUL: My mother used to make Baked Alaska.

SOPHIA: That's funny. I thought it was English but it's American?

PAUL: Yes, I guess so.

SOPHIA: Hitler is dead, isn't he?

PAUL: Yes, Hitler is dead.

SOPHIA: (*Remembering translation.*) One torture consisted in hanging the victims up by the hands...Afterwards the soles of the feet were cut with razor blades and then they were made to walk on salt.

PAUL: It's alright honey. You're safe, it's alright. You're with me, remember?

SOPHIA: I saw a woman selling garlic on the black market. 'Who will buy my Jewish onion?' she asked people. That's what she called the garlic. (*Beat.*) They still hate us. Before he died my father told me that in Palestine there is a sea so salty with the tears of all the dead that even a woman who can't swim can float on it. Even a dead woman on holiday.

PAUL: When I woke this morning, I wanted to pull you on top of me. No woman has made me feel – well, so excited.

SOPHIA: *Un coup de foudre.*

PAUL: What's that?

SOPHIA: A flash of thunder. To fall in love at first sight. I never believed in falling in love.

PAUL: And now?

SOPHIA: When I saw you in the church – of all places.

PAUL: And when I saw you in the courtroom. Working so hard, so intently. I also.

SOPHIA: I think I'm ill.

PAUL: Where?

SOPHIA: Lovesick. That's a joke for a supposedly rational woman – lovesick. It starts as a hot wave in the stomach and moves between my legs. I'm going to die with longing.

PAUL: Don't die, Sophia, not when I love you so.
(*SOPHIA and PAUL freeze in shadow. The lights come up on the GERMAN WOMAN.*)

GERMAN WOMAN: I didn't need to travel to see the world. The world was coming to me. The women from Greece travelled first class. They paid their own fares to Auschwitz and when they were about to arrive they put on make-up. The German woman does not paint her face. She is natural. She does not shave her legs. She does not smoke. Jews and gypsies, from all over they came. With all their different languages. Sometimes, in a suitcase, a baby would be found. They tried to hide these babies but we always heard them cry. You can stop an adult from crying but you can never stop a baby. Not unless you kill it. Then it stops. They blame us now but they'll soon forget. There will be other wars, others will be killed. The removal of the Jews will soon be forgotten. People will ask, why are the Jews always talking about that? Why can't they forget about it? Why can't the Jews just shut up? And our grandchildren will be tired of hearing about Jews and what was done to them. It's not our fault. Look at the Americans and what they did to the

Indians. Look at what the Americans did with the slaves. Well, the blacks are only good for work; giving them freedom was the biggest mistake. But the Jews are inferior to the Negro race. The Jews brought about the downfall of the Roman Empire. They are to blame for the Armistice of 1918 and the Versailles Treaty. All Jews are untrustworthy. It's a pity any are left alive. Hitler didn't live long enough to finish the job. They'll always cause trouble as long as they live.

Sophia's Bedroom in the Grand Hotel

Two days later.

SOPHIA: You want a vodka?

VINCENT: Where did you get vodka?

SOPHIA: From the Russians. Where did you think I got it?

VINCENT: Which Russians?

SOPHIA: Oh for God's sake, the big tall blond I slept with so I could get vodka.

VINCENT: Alright, sorry I asked.

SOPHIA: (*Lifting her skirt aggressively.*) And the stockings were from the Americans. Nylon stockings.

VINCENT: The Americans?

SOPHIA: Yes, I slept with the whole US Army.

VINCENT: Alright, alright, a joke's a joke.

SOPHIA: Only the French I didn't sleep with. I mean what can they possibly offer? The Germans took every bottle of French champagne.

VINCENT: I said alright.

SOPHIA: But of course there's no ice.

VINCENT: No ice?

SOPHIA: 'That cuts no ice with me' – you can't really translate that, you know.

VINCENT: Into French?

SOPHIA: Into French, German or English.

VINCENT: Of course you say that in English.

SOPHIA: That's because you don't even know when you speak American.

VINCENT: Is there anything you don't know?

SOPHIA: There's a lot I don't know.

VINCENT: Maybe you'll tell me one day. You know it was hard to get here. They don't allow husbands to visit their wives, not when their wives are such very important persons in this Trial. It took a lot of trouble to get here, or hadn't you realised that?

SOPHIA: I looked forward to seeing you.

VINCENT: You *looked* forward to seeing me? That's the past tense.

SOPHIA: You can't say that in French, you know. I look forward to seeing you. You have to say *J'ai hâte de te voir.* I have haste to see you. But *J'ai hâte de te voir* isn't the same. Looking forward. Maybe the French don't look forward. Maybe they live in the present and the English live in the future.

VINCENT: No, we live in the past, in the days when we had wives who loved us. (*Beat.*) What's wrong? I haven't seen you for three months and you're very strange with me. Is it the work? Is it because of the camps? I'd've shot the whole lot of them; to hell with trying them. How can you try the devil? Their names, Hess, Göring, Ribbentrop, how they stink in my mouth.

SOPHIA: What I'd really like now is some ice. Vodka cold from the fridge. It's very pure alcohol, vodka. Leaves no impurities in the system. There's no hangover. Did you know that when the Germans have strained a muscle, from too much shooting, for example, they get what they call *Muskelkarter.* Muscle hangover. Hangover, that's a good word in English. Hangover.

VINCENT: I know there's someone else, Sophia. I know you are desirable to other men. But all I ever wanted was you as my wife. Is that too much to ask? I can't stop thinking about you. And always there are other men looking. I see their eyes get excited when they look at you. Will she? That's what they're thinking. I know them. I know those men. I heard them all my life. In school, the way they looked at women in dirty

magazines. But I'm different. I just want to come home
every night and know that you're there waiting for me.
Waiting. And that there's just us. I thought that that's
how it would be between us. Us against the world. Us
locked away. Safe and cosy. You my wife. It's a lovely
word – wife. I love that word. I don't want a mistress.
I want you, my wife. Until death, you said. You were all
I wanted, Sophia. I can't stand the thought of you with
others. You don't, I know you don't. Me in England and
you in Germany, I imagine you with others. Someone
more like you. Another foreigner.
When I was at Dunkirk and the sound of their guns got
nearer and nearer, I thought of you and I wanted to get
back to you. And there was a moment when I thought,
I might die now. With the sound of the guns and the sea
and the sand all around. And if they had killed me
then, I wouldn't have minded. I had had you and that
was something I'd never ever dreamed of, a woman like
you as my wife. To have died then wouldn't have been
so bad, to have never thought of you going with
another, to have been killed before that thought, that's
not so bad, is it Sophia? (*Pause.*) I'd swing for him.

SOPHIA: What does that mean?

VINCENT: I want to kill him. And when I do, they'll hang
me. That way I'll swing for him.

SOPHIA: What are you talking about?

VINCENT: You think I don't know? You think I can't feel
someone else's fingers on your skin? You think I don't
know he's been there? In my place, in my secret place,
between your legs. I can tell, he's been there too.

SOPHIA: Oh please.

VINCENT: He's been there and I feel his presence. It's as
if we're both in you at the same time. That way I touch
him too. You made me touch him. We're not alone any
more because of him. You did that.

The Baseball Lesson

The game – stylised.

Use of whistles by players.

PAUL: Hey, kid, you want to learn a game? It's called baseball.

1ST AMERICAN: What you got to learn about baseball is that it goes real fast.

2ND AMERICAN: First you got to understand the positions. (*They run the stage to demonstrate.*)

PAUL: I'm centre fielder.

1ST AMERICAN: Left fielder.

2ND AMERICAN: Right fielder.

PAUL: Short stop.

1ST AMERICAN: First baseman.

PAUL: Second baseman.

2ND AMERICAN: Third baseman.

ALL: Pitcher.

1ST AMERICAN: Catcher.

2ND AMERICAN: Umpire.

PAUL: All you need is a bat and a ball

1ST AMERICAN: ...and gloves

2ND AMERICAN: ...and a hat to keep the sun outa your eyes

PAUL: The bat is made of wood, usually ash.

1ST AMERICAN: Now all you got to do is make sure you score more runs than the opposition.

PAUL: The batter runs when he hits the ball.

1ST AMERICAN: This gives the defenders their chance to get him out.

PAUL: If he reaches first base, his success hit is called a single.

2ND AMERICAN: If he reaches a second base, a double.

1ST AMERICAN: Third base is a triple.

PAUL: Then there are the rules.

1ST AMERICAN: The player must never rub anything on the baseball to make it do any funny tricks.

2ND AMERICAN: He must never add anything to the hitting surface of his wooden bat

PAUL: ...but the handle can be rubbed with pine tar.

1ST AMERICAN: Fielders are allowed to dive or leap for any balls including reaching among the spectators

2ND AMERICAN: ... in order to take a catch.

PAUL: The runner may employ any subterfuge such as pretending to steal a base

1ST AMERICAN: ...or trying to disturb a pitcher by jumping or walking away from his base

PAUL: ...but he must never never physically interfere with play. And remember, if there is any dispute, the umpire is always right.

1ST AMERICAN: The catcher is a real special guy.

PAUL: Not only has he got to handle each pitch any guy throws at him, he's also got to run the defence because he's the only guy with the whole field in front.

2ND AMERICAN: But the pitcher is the most specialised of all the players. The way he throws the ball

1ST AMERICAN: ...or pitch

PAUL: ...can confound the hitter.

2ND AMERICAN: He can throw a fast ball

1ST AMERICAN: ...or a screwball,

PAUL: ...a knuckler,

1ST AMERICAN: ...a slowball

2ND AMERICAN: ...or a drop.

PAUL: A really smart pitcher uses a mixture of these to surprise the guy with a bat. But the thing to remember is that every guy is both an attacker and a defender. Remember you've got to have a good arm, you've got to have speed and you've got to have judgement. Well, kid, are you ready to give it a go?

The Telephone Call

PAUL is on the phone to his wife, DEE DEE.

PAUL: Hi, can you hear me?

DEE DEE: Paul, is that you?

PAUL: Yes, Dee Dee, it's Paul.

DEE DEE: It's a good line, you could almost be in the next room.

PAUL: It's a lousy line here, I had trouble getting one.

DEE DEE: Are you in Berlin?

PAUL: No, in Nuremberg.

DEE DEE: What's it like?

PAUL: Like a graveyard, all bombed out. Except the hotel. They put us in the Grand Hotel, and that's completely untouched.

DEE DEE: And what about the Trials? Is it terrible for you doing that?

(*SOPHIA comes in and touches PAUL.*)

PAUL: Terrible. But we're moving towards a verdict.

DEE DEE: There's someone with you, I know there is.

PAUL: Yes, some guy. I borrowed his office; one of the big shots here said I could use his office for a personal call.

DEE DEE: What's his name?

PAUL: Who?

DEE DEE: This guy.

PAUL: Sophia Goldenberg.

DEE DEE: That's not a man's name.

PAUL: No, that's who he and I were talking about. Sorry, honey, this is a three-way conversation.

DEE DEE: So what's his name?

PAUL: What the hell is it to you what his name is?

DEE DEE: Paul!

PAUL: Sorry, honey, there's a lot of stress out here, you don't know what it's like having to translate this kinda stuff all day long.

DEE DEE: Do you want to talk about it?

PAUL: What now, over the phone?

SOPHIA: You're talking to your wife?

PAUL: Give me a break, will you.

DEE DEE: Paul, what's happening?

PAUL: Nothing, nothing's happening.

DEE DEE: Have you got someone there with you?

PAUL: What?

DEE DEE: Is there someone with you?

PAUL: Don't be ridiculous. Of course there's nobody with me.

SOPHIA: Why don't you tell her the truth?

PAUL: The truth — in the middle of all this, you talk to me
about the truth?

DEE DEE: There's someone there with you, isn't there?

PAUL: What?

DEE DEE: You didn't ask about the children.

PAUL: Yeah, the kids, how are they?

DEE DEE: Don't you even remember their names?

PAUL: Of course I remember their names, goddamnit.
How are Suzanne and Donald?

DEE DEE: Suzanne fell out of bed and broke her arm.

PAUL: What? She broke her arm? Why did you let her
do that?

DEE DEE: I let her do that? It was the middle of the night.
She had a nightmare. She was calling out 'Daddy,
Daddy'. She said she saw you. She said she reached out
for you. She dreamt you were lifting her up, high in the
air and that she had a big skirt on and that you were
twirling her around and around.
(*DEE DEE is crying through this.*)

PAUL: Honey, calm down, you know I can't stand it if you cry.

DEE DEE: You were twirling her around and around, she
said, and her skirt was flying everywhere. And she had
no panties on. And when she realised she had no
panties on, you dropped her.

PAUL: This was a dream, honey, the dream of a five-year-
old girl.

DEE DEE: And then you dropped her after twirling her
around and around.
(*SOPHIA screams.*)
What was that?

PAUL: What?

DEE DEE: A woman screamed.

PAUL: When?

DEE DEE: Just then.

PAUL: No.

DEE DEE: I heard her.

PAUL: I didn't hear anything.

DEE DEE: You've somebody there with you.

PAUL: No, I told you. Maybe you heard somebody out in the street.

DEE DEE: You're lying, I know you're lying.

PAUL: Come on, stop all that, you were always jealous for no reason.

DEE DEE: Someone screamed. I heard her. What was the name of that woman you mentioned before? Sophia someone.

PAUL: I have to go now. This guy wants his phone back.

DEE DEE: The guy with no name.

PAUL: I'm going now, honey.

DEE DEE: Goldenberg, that was it, wasn't it? Sophia Goldenberg?

PAUL: I said I've got to get off the line now, honey, this guy...

DEE DEE: I bet.

PAUL: Really, I've got to go, he needs to use the phone. Look, honey, there's only you, don't be so jealous. Why can't you trust me? I'm your husband, we're married, remember?

DEE DEE: Do you remember?

PAUL: I've got to go now. I'm putting the phone down now.

DEE DEE: I'm coming over to see you. I'm flying over. Paul, you can't do this to me.

PAUL: I'm putting the phone down now, honey.

DEE DEE: I mean it Paul. I'm coming to Nuremberg. I'll get there somehow.

(*PAUL hangs up. DEE DEE is left with the dialling tone. PAUL embraces SOPHIA. She holds him at arm's length after the kiss and whacks him hard on the face.*
Bring up the sound of Bach's violin concerto as the moment of rage turns into violent love.)

PAUL: What the hell am I going to do? Oh God.

SOPHIA: I don't care about your marriage. I don't care about my marriage. At this moment all that means nothing.

PAUL: I made Dee Dee a promise. Oh God, why couldn't I have met you first? I see blonde kids in the street;

they remind me of my own. And then I ask myself, did
I kill their father? I can't forget that my kids need me.

SOPHIA: You want them to know that all their childhood
you were in love with another woman?

PAUL: How will they know?

SOPHIA: Children know when their father is absent. How
can you ever be the same after this?

PAUL: Sophia?

SOPHIA: Yes?

PAUL: I don't want to lose you.

SOPHIA: And what do you suggest?

PAUL: I don't know. You bring me a whole universe.

SOPHIA: And with Dee Dee it's only America?

PAUL: I know I'm hurting you.

SOPHIA: I had a dream last night. You were burnt on the
chest. For some reason I thought of those Indian
women who are forced to be burnt alive with their dead
husbands. Well, you were burnt like that. But just the
chest. I said, Paul, you're getting better, you'll soon be
cured. You said – no, I have to die because of what
I promised my wife.

PAUL: My dreams are all of the war.

(*Pause.*)

You know I saw a wedding this morning, on my way back
to the hotel. It was out in the street. I saw this couple
being married outside because there was nowhere else
left, I guess. In France, they told me that when somebody
gets married, they leave the front door of the town hall or
the church wide open, in case someone objects; in case
the guy's already married!

SOPHIA: Why don't you just go back to what you had
before you met me?

PAUL: How can I?

SOPHIA: Yes, that's it. Go back. Forget the whole thing. You
can never leave. You're tied to your nice wife.

The Trial 3

JUDGE: The Dutch witness Vorink.

DUTCH WITNESS: I remember a mother, dragged from her home, who gave her baby to a stranger who was not a Jewess, and asked her to look after her child.

AMERICAN INTERPRETER: 'Did you or did you not know about the slave labour employed in these camps?'

GERMAN INTERPRETER: 'These were volunteers. French volunteers. And if they were forced to come, it was their own French government which forced them, not us. We treated them well.'

AMERICAN INTERPRETER: 'In Lithuania 136,421 people were liquidated in one single action.'

ENGLISH INTERPRETER: 'Germanisation of Luxembourg. The German salute will be given in the following manner:'

SOPHIA: 'a) Raise the outstretched right arm to shoulder level.

b) Shout "Heil Hitler".'

ENGLISH INTERPRETER: Hermann Göring:
'...the fabulous fertility of the Netherlands, the unique paradise that is France, Belgium too, is extraordinarily fruitful and so is the province of Posen, fertile districts of Lemberg (Lvov) and Galicia where the harvest is exceptionally good. Then comes Russia, the black earth of the Ukraine...our troops have occupied...squeeze the utmost out of them'

SOPHIA: '...that is what I expect...squeeze out of the territory now under our control with the utmost application and straining every nerve...what happens to the Frenchmen is of no importance.'

ENGLISH INTERPRETER: 'The Jewish women, when they arrived in the first months of their pregnancy, were subjected to abortion. When the pregnancy was near the end, after confinement, the babies were drowned in a bucket of water. One day, an order came from Berlin. The mothers and babies were put in a lorry and taken away to the gas chamber.'

AMERICAN TRANSLATOR: 'One torture consisted in hanging up the victims.'

JUDGE: I must ask you to slow down. I'm getting two translations at once. We have to find out who is guilty.

GERMAN INTERPRETER: *Wer ist schuldig, warum,*

JUDGE: Why.

GERMAN INTERPRETER: *...und in welcher Weise.*'

FRENCH INTERPRETER: *Qui est coupable, pourquoi et comment.*

RUSSIAN INTERPRETER: *Kto vinovat, potschemu, i kakim obrazom.*

PAUL: And when did you realise that the war was lost?

(*Crossfade to SOPHIA's hotel room. She lights two candles. She wears a headscarf.*)

SOPHIA: *Boruch ato adenoi*
elohanu melech ha ha'olom.

What comes next?

It's all gone

I will have no other gods before thee

And love?

Is that a god?

Christ, I could do with a drink

Berai peree ha goffen.

(*A memory.*) Jews are forbidden to play Bach or Brahms.

And if I do have a drink, what does that solve?

(*She pours herself a whisky.*)

Nothing, that's what it solves.

Someone once asked me – Can I live without hope? I was sixteen.

What did I know?

(*She cuts to Trial memory.*)

My name is Lampe, witness from Matthausen concentration camp. When we arrived, we were twelve hundred Frenchmen; the SS officer greeted us. He told us, 'When you enter this camp, we'll show you the road to heaven.'

(*Lighting change. SOPHIA has an hallucinatory dream. VINCENT and PAUL come into her hotel room while she is attempting to pray.*)

VINCENT: Get down. There's lead flying everywhere.

POLISH WOMAN: (*Crying.*) *Toutes les vaches sont mortes.*
  Viande bombardée.

VINCENT: *Qui êtes vous?*

POLISH WOMAN: *Polonaise. Polski.*

VINCENT: Polish?

POLISH WOMAN: *Polski.*

VINCENT: What the hell are you doing here? This isn't
  Poland, this is France. Don't you even know? *Vous êtes
  en France.*

POLISH WOMAN: *Arbeiter, Polen.*

VINCENT: A Polish slave worker, is that what you are?

POLISH WOMAN: *Toutes les vaches sont mortes.*

VINCENT: And then I saw all those young Canadians in
  a field. And she was right. They were killing them,
  killing them, killing them until the whole field was
  a heap of blood.
  And do you know why they killed them? Because the
  Germans had just killed all their regiment. That's why
  the Canadians killed the cows in the Normandy fields.
  And because there were no Germans to kill, they killed
  the cows.

PAUL: I can remember a dog being hit once in New York by
  a Cadillac. The dog wasn't hurt so bad but he was mad
  enough to bite the car.

VINCENT: I lived one day at a time. I never planned.

SOPHIA: If I live through each day I'm amazed to find
  myself alive the next morning.
  And if you are in my bed, can you be surprised that
  I never want to let you go?

GERMAN DEFENDANT: Nobody was killed because of
  my orders.

VINCENT: (*Repeating training orders.*) 'Keep one up the
  spout, push the bayonet in but not too deep. If it goes in
  too deep then use the shot for recoil and then you'll get
  it out. Keep one up the spout.'
  There were always girls. In France. I met one, she was
  friendly. She asked me to her house to have a drink. It
  looked like a château to me. I asked her about the war.
  It was 1944.

'My father and mother always entertained the Germans,' she told me. 'I suppose we'll be entertaining the English now.'

PAUL: Yes, there were always girls. But I didn't fool around too much. Cat houses, yes, sure we went there from time to time but I always ended up talking to the girls, I felt so sorry for them, and then if a guy wanted sex, there was no need to go there, there was plenty of girls ready to do it for nylons, chocolates or anything we could give them. There was a camp, we shot everyone in uniform. The Russians have got the right idea. They know all these men are guilty. They don't understand why we're going through all this to prove what we already know. I met a Russian parachutist once. She was only 15.

GERMAN DEFENDANT: We just had to piss on the Jews.

AMERICAN INTERPRETER: (*Female.*) We just had to piss on the Jews.

PAUL: I saw this Red Army soldier just staring at a heap of children's clothes.

VINCENT: Sophia, guess what I found. A man selling flowers in the middle of Nuremberg. He said he brought them from Holland. It seems people will buy flowers, even now. Here, they are for you. My mother taught me all about the different names for plants and flowers but I've forgotten them. I killed men you know, Sophia. I still see their faces. What do you do when you see your best friend robbing the dead?

JEWISH WOMAN: We sang the Marseilleise to keep our spirits up. There, in what they called 'Canada'. 'Canada' was the name of the hut where the clothes were sorted. Some were still warm.

VINCENT: It's only three weeks later that you begin to dream about what you did. You know you can be very brave running up against a beach of machine gun fire. It's only later, in dreams, that you get shot.

SOPHIA: Evidence to the court. The witness Dupont on the journey to Buchenwald...In the French convoy which left Compiègne on January 24 1944 and arrived on January 26, I saw one van containing 100 persons of which 12 were dead and eight insane. During the period of my deportation, I saw numerous transports come in. The same thing happened every time, only the numbers varied. In this way, the elimination of a certain proportion had already been achieved when the convoy arrived.

(*To PAUL.*) *Aide-moi.*

(*PAUL and SOPHIA move towards an embrace.*)

La Rencontre / The Meeting

GERMAN VOICE: Today we pronounce sentence on:

(*Gives the names of the men on trial.*)

Hermann Wilhelm Göring, Rudolf Hess, Joachim von Ribbentrop, Robert Ley, Wilhelm Keitel, Ernst Kaltenbrunner, Alfred Rosenberg, Hans Frank, Wilhelm Frick, Julius Streicher, Walter Funk, Hjalmar Schacht, Karl Doenitz, Erich Raeder, Baldur von Schirach, Fritz Sauckel, Alfred Jodl, Martin Bormann, Franz von Papen, Arthur Seyss-Inquart, Alfred Speer, Constantin von Neurath, Hans Fritzche.

(*Crossfade as PAUL exits, leaving SOPHIA and DEE DEE.*)

DEE DEE: I'm Mrs Paul Carver.

SOPHIA: Sophia Goldenberg.

DEE DEE: I'm glad to meet you. I know you are important in my husband's life.

SOPHIA: Oh yes?

DEE DEE: Shall I tell you how we met?

SOPHIA: I don't want to hear.

DEE DEE: I see.

SOPHIA: What do you see?

DEE DEE: I have two small children. Suzanne is five years old. She has blonde curly hair and large blue eyes. When she was being born, they thought I would die. She seemed to get stuck. Her birth was a terrible agony. When she arrived her face was battered, her nose was swollen, she looked as if she'd been in a fight. Paul was with me through the labour, he held my hand, and

when I felt I was going to die, I looked up at him and
I thought that as long as Paul was with me, I didn't care
if I died bearing his child. He was with me, you see, that
was all that was important. Suzanne is a very precious
child, you know, she nearly killed me, loving Paul
nearly killed me.

SOPHIA: But you lived, didn't you?

DEE DEE: Do you understand what I'm telling you?

SOPHIA: You lived. Do you know how many women died
before they knew what love is?

DEE DEE: I'm sorry. Did you have family who...

SOPHIA: Were killed by the Nazis? You can say the words,
you know.

DEE DEE: I'm sorry, I didn't mean to be insensitive.

SOPHIA: You think it's insensitive, you think anything you
can say can hurt me?

DEE DEE: I don't know. I know it's different over here in
Europe. I know you suffered in a way that we never
knew, but I read about it.

SOPHIA: You read about it.

DEE DEE: Did your family die that way?

SOPHIA: You mean gassed in Auschwitz or Treblinka?

DEE DEE: Yes.

SOPHIA: No, they put a bullet through their heads.

DEE DEE: Please. I have two small children.

SOPHIA: And I have none.

DEE DEE: But you have something which holds him the
way I can't. I can see why he loves you.

SOPHIA: What do you see?

DEE DEE: I see a beautiful, intelligent woman who has
suffered.

SOPHIA: Don't patronise me.

DEE DEE: I didn't mean to. I'm trying to understand, can't
you see that? He's all I ever had in my life...You, you've
got your career, you're attractive, you have no children,
men like you, you could have whoever you want. Go
away, find someone else, leave him, let him go.

SOPHIA: You know what strikes me? It's the thought of all
those dead young women who will never have the

pleasure of watching a lover grow old. Who will never
see the man they love at forty, at fifty, at sixty. Will never
see his firm skin gradually turn to fine pleats. Will never
experience the sweet, sweet sensation of loving that
skin year after year. Or watching a lover in the bath and
washing him all over as if that soft-skinned, soapy man
were her own child. Will never have the pleasure of
being a young girl still, under her own mature skin.
Of stretching a hand out under the sheets and knowing
that she's chosen this man of all men; this man to
cherish in the dark nights when hell is outside. I don't
think of the youth that was stolen. I think of the lost joy
of growing old, of the possibility of love in age. Of
loving someone whose hair is grey and seeing the boy
of eighteen in the man of sixty or seventy. That's what
I miss when I think of Dachau. Or Auschwitz.

DEE DEE: Let me have him back.

La Rencontre 2 / The Verdict

JUDGE: One thing we can be sure, they have been given
the kind of trial they never gave any man.

DEE DEE: I'm Mrs Paul Carver.

VINCENT: My darling Sophia.

GERMAN WOMAN: Göring cheated them. They
thought they could hang him but he cheated them.
He took poison.

DEE DEE: Mrs Paul Carver.

JUDGE: Göring was half militarist, half gangster.

GERMAN WOMAN: They don't realise that we are cleverer
than them. They think we're going to wait for a hanging.
Göring wasn't a criminal. He was a patriot.

VINCENT: He went back to America you know, with
his wife.

DEE DEE: Mrs Paul Carver.

VINCENT: I must know where you are and that you are
still alive.

JUDGE: Streicher, the venomous vulgarian, manufactured
and distributed obscene racial libels.

GERMAN WOMAN: Göring was a Renaissance man. He loved music. There was so much music in the camps.

VINCENT: I want you to come back to me. I forgive you. These things happen. We can start a new life.

JUDGE: And Funk, as Reichsbank President, banked for the SS the gold teeth fillings of concentration camp victims – probably the most ghoulish collateral in banking history.

VINCENT: When you disappeared, I looked all over Nuremberg for you. I met him. He's a fine man. He said he loved you and that both hurt and pleased me. You are a woman men love.

DEE DEE: Mrs Paul Carver.

GERMAN WOMAN: We got the Jews to play for us. And we got them to play for each other when the trains arrived full, we gave them Strauss, we gave them Mozart, we gave them Bach.

JUDGE: If we combine the stories from the front bench, this is the ridiculous composite picture of Hitler's government that emerges. It was composed of a number two man, Göring, who 'knew nothing of the excesses of the Gestapo' which he created, and 'never suspected the Jewish extermination programme' although he was the signer of over a score of decrees.

VINCENT: I showed your picture to other blokes and I could see they were jealous. How could a fella like me get a girl like you? And I never knew why you chose me.

GERMAN WOMAN: What we should have done is send the Jews to France. The French are stinking lazy, like the Poles. The Jews aren't lazy, they work and we made them work even harder.

JUDGE: Hess, a number three man who was 'merely an innocent middleman transmitting Hitler's orders, without even reading them', like a postman or a delivery boy.

VINCENT: I want you to come back to me.

DEE DEE: Mrs Paul Carver.

VINCENT: I want you to love me again. He was never free.

JUDGE: Ribbentrop, a Foreign Minister, who knew nothing of foreign affairs.

GERMAN WOMAN: This judge, this American Jackson, I bet he's really a Jew.

JUDGE: Keitel, a Field Marshal, who issued orders to the armed forces but had no idea of the results they would have.

GERMAN WOMAN: He's probably Jacobson, and this Shawcross, from England – what's his background?

JUDGE: Rosenberg, a Party philosopher who was interested in historical research but had no idea of the violence which his philosophy was inciting in the twentieth century.

Frank, a Governor General of Poland; von Schirach, a *Gauleiter* of Vienna, a Reichsbank President who was totally ignorant of what went in and out of the vaults of his bank, and Schacht, a Plenipotentiary for War Economy who secretly marshalled the entire economy for armament but had no idea it had anything to do with war.

DEE DEE: I read about it. It's not my fault what happened over there.

JUDGE: If you were to say of these men that they are not guilty, it would be as true to say there had been no war, there have been no slain, there has been no crime.

GERMAN WOMAN: They think they can hang us or put us out of jobs but there are too many of us to hang. We can wait until we are united again. We'll hide. You see we've got to finish the job. There is always more work to do. We have to give work to our own people, not to dirty foreigners. There is so much industry to make work again.

And while I'm waiting I'm going to make sure everyone knows who is a Jew and a useless eater. They can change their names but I'll find them. They won't get away from me this time. Oh no.

(*Against this speech play the American, French, British and French national anthems using the cast to symbolise the Allies.*

*Hold on PAUL, SOPHIA, VINCENT and DEE DEE in
separate spots.
Spot on the shape of the GERMAN WOMAN smoking a
cigarette. Let the smoke be prominent as a reminder of the
smoke of six million.
PAUL and SOPHIA move towards one another as the lights
fade to blackout.)*

The End.

THE DYBBUK

Dedicated to the memory of
Rabbi Hugo Gryn

Characters

JUDITH
a modern Jewish British woman.
She becomes RACHEL in the ghetto
and plays LEAH in *The Dybbuk*

DAVID plays HANAN, NACHMAN, a BEGGAR
and the RABBI in *The Dybbuk*

JAN plays NISSAN, a JEWISH STUDENT, the RABBI
and MENACHE in *The Dybbuk*

NAOMI plays the MESSENGER, SENDER
and a BEGGAR in *The Dybbuk*

ESTHER plays the STORYTELLER
and a WOMAN in *The Dybbuk*

The Dybbuk was first produced at the New End Theatre on 25 June 1992, with the following cast:

JUDITH/RACHEL, Kate Margam

DAVID, Phillippe Smolikowski

JAN, Thomas Kampe

NAOMI, Nicky Goldie

ESTHER, Ruth Lass

Director, Julia Pascal

Lighting Design, Ian Watts

Design and movement, Thomas Kampe

Original music, Kyla Greenbaum

Sound design, Colin Brown

Acknowledgements:

Thanks to Thomas Kampe for the German translation and to Alain Carpentier for the French translation.

Scene 1

Lights up on JUDITH.

The rest of the company have their backs to the audience. They are dressed in 1940s costumes. She is dressed in today's casual clothes.

JUDITH: I was in Germany and they went on strike. Not because of me. It was nothing to do with me. A little holiday with my fiancé combined with a little research for my job.
Satellite communication.
It was a hot spring day in Frankfurt. In the park by the Opera House, just by Goethe's statue, two hundred young people were shooting-up. We were walking hand in hand. And suddenly we were in Dante's inferno.
They were burning stuff, snorting stuff, injecting stuff. It was a kind of communal mass. One girl filled her vein with heroin and then passed on the syringe to another young woman. I wanted to shout, 'Stop, don't take it.' But she was past knowing anything.
I took trains in the strike. There were no trams or buses but the trains still ran on time. To. The. Second.
Strange things happen to me on trains. I meet men. Of a certain age. Men who have not enjoyed the mercy of a late birth. For some strange reason, they are always drawn to me. They are curious. They ask me something in German and when I respond they tell me my German is good and where did I learn it. From my grandmother, I say. Was she German? No, Romanian. Then I wait. Shall I pretend she was a Christian? I can't. (*Pause.*) She also spoke Yiddish. (*Beat.*)
Then they look at me hard. There is usually a silence. Maybe they talk about something else, the strike, what a pity it is that there is no Berlin Wall, the invasion of all those East Germans, anything to cover what is going on behind their eyes. And then little by little it comes out.

'I knew about the Jews. Yes, I knew. I even helped them.
My mother lived on the Dutch border. She heard the
trains. She used to go out when it was a new moon, in
order not to be seen, you understand. She went out
and picked up all the scraps of paper, the tiny messages
that the people threw out. They wrote on anything,
a label from a jacket, a handkerchief, any scrap of
material would do. The messages were to warn children
in hiding. Of course we collected all these messages
and filled up our kitchen table with them. We tried
to get messages to those hidden children. We did what
we could.'
They don't always pretend to have helped. Maybe that
man did help. How do I know? Sometimes they tell
me of their life in the Hitler Youth. Of their joy in
pointing out a Jew hiding a yellow star behind an empty
briefcase. Of Jews riding in trams refusing to ride in the
Jews' car.
I go to Germany and I think that Hitler won. Where is
my generation? Where are my cousins?
Where is the dream of assimilation? Oh yes, Hitler
won. In Heidelberg, just by McDonalds, is the square
where they rounded up the Jews. I see a man in
a *yamulka*. He wears the mark of a religious Jew
in defiance.
Somehow he embarrasses me. As so many religious Jews
do. Am I ashamed to be a Jew? Is this my own self-hatred?
My own anti-Semitism? I don't even believe in God, so
what makes me a Jew? They don't talk of such things in
my family. Keep your head down. Be British, be cool, be
part of the crowd.
More and more I think about my family who vanished.
I wonder what happened to them.
I imagine them in a ghetto in Vilna or maybe in Warsaw
or Lodz. I know it sounds strange but I am haunted by
faces, different accents, different bodies, all the lost
cousins and aunts and uncles who I want to have
known.

I see a blonde woman, a dark man, a curly-haired redhead, a fair young man. I don't know who they are but they often come to me in dreams. They say that a person can be filled with the soul of another and that soul, which has died too early, is a dybbuk, but I, I, I have so many dybbuks.

(*Lighting change.*

Actors slowly turn around. They are carrying suitcases in their arms. Slowly they let the cases fall to reveal yellow stars on their left breast.)

Scene 2
The Ghetto

They are quietly singing 'Alexander's Ragtime Band' and playing cards. NAOMI is putting on lipstick.

RACHEL: When the *Titanic* went down they were playing Alexander's Ragtime Band.

NAOMI: It's a good song.

RACHEL: Where did you get lipstick?

NAOMI: I found it.

ESTHER: I'm hungry.

NAOMI: You want to eat this, lipstick's very good for you.

RACHEL: Stop it.

JAN: Leave her alone will you.

DAVID: Madame thinks she's the Queen of England.

JAN: Don't be silly there isn't a Queen, there's a King. The Queen of England is just a little girl.

NAOMI: Queen Marie of Romania; she was English royalty you know. The English know all about royalty.
Oh yes, Queen Marie was English. Queen Victoria's granddaughter. Her son King Carol had a mistress.

RACHEL: How do you know that?

ESTHER: Madame Lupescu.

RACHEL: How did you know?

NAOMI: I shouldn't be here. I'm only half Jewish. My father was a Jew, it's true, but not my mother. She is

a pure Aryan. From Berlin she was. (*Looks at the lipstick.*)
A good German woman does not use make-up, she
doesn't drink, she doesn't smoke. I shouldn't be here.
It's a mistake. Let me go home, please let me go home.
I hate this place. I hate being here. I hate being Jewish.
I hate being Jewish.

(*RACHEL slaps her to stop the hysteria.*)

RACHEL: That's better, isn't it? A good slap is what you
need. Now let's talk about being half Jewish. Which
half is it? The lower or the upper? Or are you divided
laterally? Which half of your brain is Jewish? The right
or the left lobe? The rational or the irrational?

DAVID: That's enough. Leave her alone.

RACHEL: Why? Are you half Jewish also? Are you the same
as her?

DAVID: I said leave her alone. We're all on edge.

NAOMI: Madame Lupescu was a Jew. So we're related
to royalty.

RACHEL: Through the bed.

JAN: My mother always said my father used her like a toilet.

NAOMI: Don't dishonour the name of your mother, may
she rest in peace.

DAVID: The rabbis say a woman is entitled to pleasure from
her husband.

ESTHER: I'm hungry.

JAN: We're all hungry.

RACHEL: The rabbis hate women.

NAOMI: Here she goes again with her crackpot ideas.

DAVID: How can you say that?

JAN: I once heard a story about Hulda.

ESTHER: Hulda was a rabbi's wife. She was so clever that
all the people came to her rather than her husband for
advice. So he set a trap.

DAVID: What sort of a trap?

ESTHER: He arranged for his most beautiful pupil, a
young man with large black eyes and an angular face,
to go privately to Hulda every day. Every day he was to
speak sweetly to her.

NAOMI: I'm hungry.

DAVID: Think about something else.

ESTHER: Every day he was to charm her with his soft hands and his honey voice, and do you know what he did to win her?

JAN: Brought her chocolate.

ESTHER: He made her laugh.

NAOMI: Ha ha ha.

JAN: What happened?

ESTHER: She was tempted.

RACHEL: She was tempted.

DAVID: They slept together.

ESTHER: And the rabbi, her husband, said, 'See how weak she is, she doesn't deserve her reputation.'

RACHEL: Ah but did she enjoy it?

JAN: Why do you always have to interrupt?

ESTHER: So the rabbis discussed it and instead of blaming the wife they blamed her husband for putting temptation in her way.

NAOMI: I would have divorced him and set up with the beautiful young man.

(*Pause.*)

JAN: What if I made a run for it?

DAVID: They will shoot you in the back.

ESTHER: And if we stay they will take us away like cattle.

DAVID: I'm cold.

NAOMI: I'm hungry.

RACHEL: Think of something else.

JAN: I can't stop thinking about food.

RACHEL: I told you, think about something else.

JAN: Like what?

DAVID: The Queen of Sheba?

JAN: Women.

DAVID: That's another kind of hunger.

RACHEL: The Queen of Sheba was invited to a banquet with King Solomon. He wanted to spend the night with her but she was too proud. 'I'm the Queen of Sheba,' she said. 'I'm certainly not going to consort

with you.' He said, 'Come and banquet with me and
then we'll lie in each other's arms.'
He said, 'I'll make a bargain with you. You dine with me
and sleep in my special chamber for honoured guests
but if you take anything from my palace then you will
sleep in my arms.'

DAVID: I once ate a piece of lamb so pink in the middle
that it made me think I was eating nirvana.

NAOMI: What do you know of nirvana, are you a Buddhist?

ESTHER: You mean a Hindu.

NAOMI: Miss Know-It-All.

JAN: This banquet – what did they eat?

RACHEL: Fish, smoked and salted fish, herrings.

NAOMI: Don't be silly.

JAN: White, white bread with butter, pale butter and
cheese.

DAVID: Duck – the breast; no, the leg.

NAOMI: Stuffed peppers. Peppers stuffed with meat and
set on a bed of rice with a special sauce. Mushrooms,
wild mushrooms.

RACHEL: Braised fennel in butter with thin slices of veal.

JAN: Poppy seed cake.

ESTHER: Ice-cream, chocolate ice-cream.

RACHEL: The meal was very salty, salted fish, salted meat.

NAOMI: I'm only a half-Jew. Oh God help me, I shouldn't
be here.
(*Silence.*)

DAVID: We haven't talked about the wine. A good French
wine?

ESTHER: A Sylvaner from Alsace.

DAVID: Vodka, lots and lots of vodka.

RACHEL: The meal was highly spiced with chillies and
pimentos. That night —

DAVID: They took my parents away in the night. I was
working in the hospital. I came back early in the
morning. Their bed was still indented with their
shape. I put my hand into the bed to feel the sheets.
The sheets were still warm.

ESTHER: Red or green peppers?
(*Next line is delivered very fast to block out her reaction to DAVID's memory.*)
You have to lightly plunge them in hot water to soften them before you stuff them.
RACHEL: That night, the Queen of Sheba went to bed in the guest's chamber and she awoke dying of thirst.
ESTHER: You have to buy the wide peppers, they are better than the long ones.
RACHEL: So she called for her servant to bring her a glass of water.
ESTHER: My grandmother always made a boiling chicken with the eggs.
RACHEL: And Solomon was hiding behind a curtain. And when he heard her call for water he said, 'Ah, madame, you want something from my palace, you want to drink water from my house.'
And, when she saw him, she was so thirsty that she begged for the water.
NAOMI: And in return she spent the night with him.
RACHEL: Am I telling this story or are you?
ESTHER: They say that somewhere, in Ethiopia, there are black Jews.
DAVID: I'd like to see them.
NAOMI: This lipstick is finished.
(*She throws it away. JAN retrieves it.*)
What do you want that for?
RACHEL: He's going to give it to the Queen of Sheba.
JAN: Or Princess Elizabeth.
DAVID: Yes, you could marry her and then you'd be the King of England and eat bacon and eggs.
JAN: Black pudding.
RACHEL: Knuckle of pork.
DAVID: Very kosher.
ESTHER: They make a sweet pudding with rice.
NAOMI: They have their Blackshirts too.
DAVID: The British would not put us in a ghetto.
RACHEL: Of course they wouldn't. (*Beat.*)
They wouldn't let us in in the first place.

DAVID: My father wanted me to go to England.

NAOMI: London. Paris. Rome. Vienna. Venice. Berlin...
When this is all over I want to see those cities. I want to
go there with someone I love. To a little hotel with clean
sheets. To walk hand in hand through the city and
never see a swastika. Just like it was before.

JAN: Hickory dickory dock, the mouse ran up the clock
and said what a good boy am I.

NAOMI: You've mixed it up.

DAVID: My mother —

RACHEL: Don't talk about it.

DAVID: (*To RACHEL.*) You think my mother and your
mother are together?

RACHEL: I said don't talk about it.

NAOMI: My mother was a Christian.

JAN: My mother was as blonde as an Aryan goddess. My
father was as fair as her. They had forgotten they were
Jews. They believed they were Protestants. Every
morning I said the Lord's Prayer.

NAOMI: They took my parents and my 10-year-old sister.
I came back from the factory. You see, I used to be at the
university until they threw us all out. I got a job in the
factory making leather bags.
I had been working all night. I got back at six in the
morning. When they came back for me, I took her coat.
And in the pocket was a lipstick. It's all I have of her.
(*JAN looks at the lipstick.*)
I know they are dead.

JAN: How do you know? You never know.

ESTHER: Until you see their bodies.

DAVID: You think they are going to send them back for an
identity parade?

RACHEL: For God's sake.

NAOMI: I don't think God comes in to it.

JAN: I never thought God came in to it and still they tell
me I'm a Jew.

ESTHER: You are a Jew.

JAN: Thank you, do I need you to remind me? (*Beat.*)
You think someone would like to buy a lipstick.

RACHEL: Sell it to Buckingham Palace when you next visit.

ESTHER: (*To NAOMI.*) How did you get to the ghetto?

NAOMI: Well, it wasn't in a taxi.

(*Sounds of 'heraus' being shouted, the group freeze, stylised moment when the Nazis raid the ghetto for a transport to Auschwitz. All that is heard after the sound is the breathing of the group.*
Light change. JAN starts singing, the group join in. It is a Yiddish Resistance song, the melody from the Vilna Partisans Song.
NAOMI throws herself on the floor in hysteria.)

RACHEL: Stop it. You're alive another day, aren't you? Stop it now.

(*DAVID takes NAOMI's hand and tries to soothe her. RACHEL bursts out into terrible laughter, JAN continues the Resistance song.*)

ESTHER: Stop that laughing — it sounds like you're a dybbuk.

RACHEL: Look, here's my mother's dress. I found something sewn in the lining.

(*She takes out a diamond ring and holds it to the light.*)

I knew what it meant. It was her engagement ring.

DAVID: (*Mocking her.*) So you really are a princess, you've got a diamond ring.

RACHEL: I made my own living you know. My parents had no money. Nobody ever kept me like a princess. I sewed corsets and bras for rich ladies.

JAN: How many of us do you think they've taken?

NAOMI: Oh God, oh God

RACHEL: Oh my God, (*Irony.*) why hast thou forsaken me?

ESTHER: Does anybody believe in God?

ESTHER: Why are we Jews if we don't believe in God?

NAOMI: Because they tell us we're Jews.

ESTHER: Once upon a time, there were two Chassidic Jews, two friends —

RACHEL: They are coming back, they are coming back!

JAN: No they are not, they have their quota.

RACHEL: Where is my mother, where is my father? Where are my brothers and sisters, where is my fiancé?

JAN: I will be your fiancé.

NAOMI: Mother.

DAVID: I will be your fiancé, if you would like that.

NAOMI: Once upon a time, go on...

ESTHER: There were two men who were great friends, two Chassidim —

RACHEL: Oh for God's sake, can't we ever be free of religious Jews?

ESTHER: Don't talk like that, that's how *they* talk.

NAOMI: I like their music.

JAN: They don't help us. They don't assimilate. They are stuck in the Middle Ages.

ESTHER: They die like us.

(*Pause.*)

RACHEL: What's your story?

ESTHER: (*As STORYTELLER.*) Once upon a time in an old synagogue in a small Polish Lithuanian *shtetl* in Russia there was a young man called Hanan. A studious young man who fasted six whole days a week.

DAVID: Isn't that what we're doing?

(*Lights change as the play is enacted.*)

ESTHER: (*As STORYTELLER.*) But before we get to the young man's story we have to go back twenty years. Two friends, Nissan and Sender, (*She puts hats on the heads of JAN and NAOMI.*) made a promise. They loved one another very much. (*She makes NAOMI and JAN hug.*) Now one day both men, Sender (*NAOMI.*) and Nissan, (*JAN.*) realised that both their wives were pregnant and they made a pledge. If one had a girl and one had a boy, then the two children would reflect the love of their fathers and would marry. And when the babies were born, Sender was father to a girl – Leah and Nissan to a boy – Hanan. But one day Nissan drowned and the poor boy Hanan was forced to make his own living as soon as he could. He mended shoes and also studied. He became the best student in the *yeshiva* – that's the school where boys study – and one day, he started walking, something made him walk and walk until he found what he was looking for. Some unknown force

took him to the small town of Brainitz. Out in the street
he saw a young girl. And when he saw her he had a
sudden pain in his heart. A feeling that he had known
this unknown girl all his life. And that without her he
could not live. And he followed her only to find that she
was the daughter of the richest merchant in the town –
Sender. He wanted to marry Leah but of course he had
no money to honour the contract. Hanan was rich in
intelligence but not in gold.

DAVID: (As HANAN. *Quoting the Kabbalah.*) It's simple. The
chair is not a chair. The orchestra is not an orchestra.
Horses are not horses. Everything is appearance.
And we are merely strangers on the earth.

ESTHER: (*To JAN.*) Now you play a young student.

JAN: (As *1ST STUDENT.*) I could do with a drink. It's a pity
your rabbi isn't here to offer us a drop of wine. Like you,
I've fasted all day and a taste of wine would sweeten
my sleep.

ESTHER: Rachel, you play a second student. A boy.

RACHEL: Thank you God for not making me a woman.

ESTHER: Do you want the role or not?

RACHEL: I'll do it.

JAN: (As *1ST STUDENT.*) I said I could do with a drink.

RACHEL: (As *2ND STUDENT.*) Don't worry, you'll soon be
drinking your fill. Sender is about to marry off his
daughter Leah.

DAVID: (As HANAN.) What?

RACHEL: (As *2ND STUDENT.*) And, as soon as the contract is
signed, you'll drink like Jonah before he met the whale.

DAVID: (As HANAN.) What?

RACHEL: (As *2ND STUDENT.*) Don't worry, he'll never sign.
The contract's never enough for him. Three times he's
turned down a suitable offer; three times he's haggled
over the price.

DAVID: (As HANAN.) In the past when a rich man went in
search of a suitable match for his daughter, he gave the
rabbi a beautiful gift and the rabbi presented him with
his best pupil.

ESTHER: Enter the Messenger.

NAOMI: (*As MESSENGER.*) Sender could find the best match here, in this synagogue.

RACHEL: (*As 2ND STUDENT.*) Oh? They say a fiancé is always predestined.

ESTHER: (*As STORYTELLER.*) A door opens. A woman and a little girl enter.

(*As the WOMAN.*) Oh help me, please help me. Before the holy books I implore you. God of Abraham and of Isaac, help my granddaughter, don't take away her mother. Listen to my cries, I will pierce the heavens with my cries, my daughter is dying, please, please don't let her die.

JAN: (*As RABBI.*) Hana-Esther, find 10 Jews to pray for the health of your daughter.

RACHEL: What good will that do?

(*During the next speech, the actors crudely mime the scenario.*)

NAOMI: (*As MESSENGER.*) This widow has been here for the past 10 days in her fight against death. And this morning another woman came for help because her daughter has been struggling to give birth for 10 days. If the sick woman dies then the baby of the other woman can be born. But if she recovers, then the baby will be born dead.

DAVID: (*As HANAN.*) And my Leah? Oh holy books, help me to get my Leah. How can I have a sign? Nine books of truth. Each book is made of the four trees of life. Once more, nine fours are 36. What's the meaning of 36? Once more I am confronted by this number without knowing its meaning. Thirty-six is the number of letters in Leah's name. Three times 36 is the number of letters in my name – Hanan. Le – a , that means without God. What a terrible thought but how fascinating.

JAN: (*As 1ST STUDENT.*) You study Kabbalah?

DAVID: (*As HANAN.*) Kabbalah. How Kabbalah enchants me; it delights the soul and leads it to paradise.

JAN: (*As 1ST STUDENT.*) You worry me. It's easy to lose your footing and slide into danger. The Talmud keeps you

on the right path but the Kabbalah can lead who knows where.
(*During the next speech, DAVID/HANAN and JAN/1ST STUDENT wrestle.*)

DAVID: (*As HANAN.*) What do we know of men? Maybe we need to follow our curiosity. Happiness is purity of the soul. Sin stands on the doorstep, as it says in Genesis. When a soul becomes pure, another soul, a soul also touched by sin, replaces it. One generation repents and the next generations are strengthened by their fathers' repentance.

RACHEL: I saw a Nazi shoot a Jew in the street. A little girl ran towards him and screamed at him. She was only about five. She smacked his legs in anger. The Nazi lifted up the little girl and laughed at her sense of injustice. And she, the little girl, did not know whether to be comforted by the big man who was her daddy or to smack him again and again.

NAOMI: What did she do?

RACHEL: I don't know. Somebody pushed me away.

DAVID: (*As HANAN. Dragging the action back.*) Less and less does each generation resist the temptation of evil.

JAN: (*As 1ST STUDENT.*) There is no holiness in sin.

DAVID: (*As HANAN.*) Everything God created is saintly.

RACHEL: Even Hitler?

JAN: Satan created Hitler, not God.

DAVID: And who created Satan but God? Satan is the opposite of God but he is also part of God and therefore partly holy.

JAN: Satan holy! I don't think so, no, I can't accept that. But would it be a sin to kill Hitler?

NAOMI: I could kill Hitler.

RACHEL: I could kill Hitler.

ESTHER: Thou shalt not kill.

JAN: Even Hitler?

ESTHER: Even Hitler.

RACHEL: Turn the other cheek?

ESTHER: But to kill when you've seen so much killing...

RACHEL: And if you saw Hitler's men killing your beloved?

(*Pause.*)
ESTHER: I would kill.
(*Pause.*
Music.
DAVID drags the action back to 'The Dybbuk'.)
DAVID: (*As HANAN.*) Which is the most powerful of
sins, the most difficult of all sins — isn't it desire for
a woman?
JAN: (*As 1ST STUDENT.*) Yes.
NAOMI: (*As MESSENGER.*) Enter Leah shyly.
RACHEL: (*As LEAH. To HANAN.*) You promised to show me
the ancient, embroidered curtains in this synagogue.
(*DAVID/HANAN gazes at RACHEL/LEAH.*)
RACHEL: (*As LEAH.*) I've never been here at night. At night
the synagogue is full of dead souls who come to pray. Old
synagogues are stained with the tears of the dead, those
who died before their time.
NAOMI: (*Shivers.*) Enough of the dead, let's get on with
the living.
RACHEL: (*As LEAH.*) It's sad here but somehow I like it.
I want to stay here. I want to hug the walls and ask them
why they are so desolate like my heart, cut apart by
sadness and tenderness. (*Looking at DAVID/HANAN.*)
JAN: (*To NAOMI.*) Who are you?
NAOMI: I'm the Messenger.
DAVID: What messenger?
NAOMI: You know, like in the Greek plays. Haven't you
read Euripides or Sophocles?
DAVID: Of course. We studied Greek at medical school
before they threw out the Jews.
NAOMI: Like in *Oedipus* when the Messenger tells the
audience that Oedipus is going to marry his mother.
(*As MESSENGER.*) Who is that young man who cannot
take his eye off you?
RACHEL: (*As LEAH.*) Hanan, a young student. He has
dined at our table. Hanan, why are you so sad, so pale?
You look ill.
DAVID: (*As HANAN.*) Come to me, my sister, my love
Your lips are bright ruby

Your mouth is all charm
Behind your veil your cheek is like a pomegranate.

NAOMI: (*As MESSENGER.*) They say that a fiancé has to be predestined.

JAN: (*As 1ˢᵀ STUDENT.*) Hanan! Sender cannot marry off his daughter so quickly. They still argue about the dowry! (*DAVID/HANAN cries out with joy.*)

NAOMI: (*As MESSENGER.*) Let's drink and celebrate. (*The group dance to the melody of 'What can you mach in America?' ESTHER starts to sing along and the others join in. There is mock Chassidic dancing and JAN plays an imaginary violin.*)

ESTHER: (*Mid-song.*) Stop. We can't celebrate. Sender just signed a marriage contract with a rich man's son in the neighbouring village.

RACHEL: But that's not clear.

NAOMI: You should have told us earlier.

ESTHER: Not all stories are told in a straight line you know. You learn them gradually.

JAN: It was a hot afternoon. I was just sixteen and coming home from school. There was a woman next to me. She wasn't young but she had a lushness about her. A kind of shabby beauty. Her packages were half on the seat, so she took up a lot of room. I could feel the warmth of the unknown woman's leg against my own. The bus crawled, the roads were dusty. Everyone and everything was half asleep. And I, too, fell into a half-sleep and, as I did, I was aware of the woman's leg against mine. I didn't look at her face and, as the bus crawled along the slow-moving street, back to my part of town, I was absorbed by the incredible heat of her body. I didn't know whether to move my leg, to acknowledge the distance of complete strangers, or to allow it to remain against hers and she, half asleep, didn't move away. When we reached the terminus I got up and avoided her face. I didn't want her to see that my cheeks were burning. (*Sound of whistle from outside.*)

NAOMI: Shush. Something's happening. (*A silence as everyone freezes listening to sounds outside. A baby's cry breaks the silence.*)

ESTHER: Let's get back to the story.

NAOMI: No, no, I've had enough. I can't go on. I can't go on.
(*Pause. DAVID forces the action back.*)

DAVID: (*As HANAN.*) The contract signed. How is that possible? So everything was for nothing, the fasting, the prayers, the ritual baths. What can I do now? What path will I follow? Ah ah ah. I understand now. I will do it.

ESTHER: (*As MESSENGER. To NAOMI/SENDER.*) Are you sure you are in total harmony with the marriage?

NAOMI: I told you I've had enough.

ESTHER: Please, Naomi. Be Leah's father. Be Sender. We don't have enough men. Please.
(*NAOMI takes the hat unwillingly.*)
(*As MESSENGER.*) Are you sure you are in total harmony with this marriage?

NAOMI: (*As SENDER. Frightened.*) Yes.
(*As herself.*) Are you the Messenger now?

ESTHER: Well, you can't play both, can you?

NAOMI: But I liked playing the Messenger best.

ESTHER: (*As MESSENGER.*) Sender. About this marriage you are organising. What if one of the parties has not kept his word? Be careful.

NAOMI: (*As SENDER.*) Who are you? I don't know you.
(*To others.*) Who is this?
(*As herself. With irony.*) Bring out the wine, let's celebrate, we've a wedding to come.

ESTHER: (*As MESSENGER.*) One day a rich, avaricious Chassid went to see the rabbi. The rabbi showed the Chassid a window. 'Look,' he said, 'and tell me what you see.'

NAOMI: (*As SENDER.*) I see people.

ESTHER: (*As MESSENGER.*) Then the rabbi led him to a mirror. 'And now what do you see?'

NAOMI: (*As SENDER.*) I see myself.

ESTHER: (*As MESSENGER.*) 'Don't you understand?' asked the rabbi. 'Both the mirror and the window are made of glass but behind the mirror is a painted layer of silver. And when there is a layer of silver, then a man stops seeing the lives of others and sees only himself.'

NAOMI: (*As SENDER.*) I said, let's dance. My daughter is to be married. Why shouldn't I dance?
(*Crossfade to DAVID/HANAN. Lighting change.*)

DAVID: (*As HANAN.*) And God created us as male and female, the perfect fusion of both. Female is intelligence. Male is wisdom. Oh come to me, my sister, my love. Male and female, we. (*Beat.*) A miniature of the universe, of the tree of life. An immense tree of life and the branches reached out into the heavens and its roots grew deep into the soil and this tree of life, the soul, is wrapped in an envelope of flesh, an envelope of flesh which is predestined for another. And before they descend from the heavens, these souls unite with one another to make one unity. It's only when they descend to earth that they separate into two different bodies. A woman's and a man's. That is how special couples are made; made in heaven before birth, and marriage ensures that these souls find each other on earth.
(*DAVID/HANAN falls and dies.*
RACHEL/LEAH screams.)

RACHEL: (*As LEAH.*) Oh no. Don't leave me.
(*Kaddish is said by ESTHER while the others 'bury' DAVID/HANAN. As RACHEL speaks, JAN and ESTHER speak fragments in German and French respectively. Translations in both languages follow this speech.*) A man is made to enjoy a long life and if he dies before he has lived, where is his soul? Once upon a time, there was a young man and he had a great spirit, he was a profound thinker, and suddenly, without warning, the thread of his life is broken, he is a stranger in a strange land. Where are the words he will never speak? Where are the children he will never have? When a candle burns out we light another one but when a life is gone? (*Beat.*) If a man dies too soon, his soul returns to know the joys and sufferings that were his due.
At night, after midnight, poor souls come to the synagogue to pray. There is a world which mirrors

our world. A world apart. And there exist forests and
meadows, oceans and deserts, towns and villages. The
deserts are whipped apart by storms, sharks patrol the
oceans and in the forests anguish, pain and death fill
the air. There is only one thing missing in this
subterranean world: the sky with its flashes and its sun.
The Talmud is like this skyless world. It is immense
but it chains us to the earth. It stops us daring to find
other worlds. But the Kabbalah, it ravishes the soul
and carries it off to the heavenly palace.

JAN: *Der Mensch soll sich an einem langen Leben erfreuen, und
wenn er stirbt bevor er gelebt hat, wo ist dann seine Seele? Es
war einmal ein junger Mann von Geist, der war ein grosser
Denker, und plötzlich, ohne Warnung, wird der Faden seines
Lebens zerissen: er ist ein Frender in einem frenden Land. Wo
sind die Worte die er nie sprechen wird? Wo sind die Kinder die
er nie haben wird? Wenn eine Kerze verbrennt zuenden wir eine
Neue an, aber wenn unser Leben erlischt? Wenn ein Mensch zu
früh stirbt, kehrt seine Seele zurück, um all die Freuden und
Leiden, die sie nie kennengelernt hat, zu erfahren. Nachts, nach
Mitternacht, kehren arme Seelen in die Synagoge zurück um zu
beten. Es gibt eine Welt die unsere Welt widerspiegelt. Eine weit
entfernte Welt. Und dort gibt es Wälder und Wiesen, Ozeane und
Wüsten, Dörfer und Städte. Die Wüsten werden von Stürmen
auseinander gepeitscht, Haifische patrolieren die Ozeane und
in den Wäldern herrschen Angst, Schmerz und der Tod. In dieser
unterirdischen Welt fehlt nue eins: der Himmel mit seinen
Blitzen un der Sonne. Der Talmud ist wie diese himmelose Welt.
Er hindert uns daran andere Welten zu suchen. Aber die
Kabbalah verzehrt die Seele und trägt sie hoch in die
himmlischen Paläste.*

ESTHER: *Un homme doit jouir d'une vie longue et s'il meurt trop
tôt, où est son âme? Il était une fois, un jeune homme de grand
esprit, c'était un penseur profond, et, brusquement, sans
avertissement, le fil de sa vie s'est cassé, il est devenu un
étranger dans un pays étranger. Où sont les mots qu'il n'a
jamais prononcés? Où sont les enfants qu'il n'a jamais eus?
Quant une bougie s'éteint, on en allume une autre mais quand*

une vie s'en va…Si un homme meurt trop tôt, son âme revient
pour connaître les joies et les souffrances qui lui sont dues. La
nuit, après minuit, de pauvres âmes viennent à la synagogue
pour prier. Et là, il existe un monde à l'image de notre monde.
Un monde à part. Et là, il existe des forêts et des champs, des
océans et des déserts, des villes et des villages. Les déserts sont
balayés par des tempêtes; des requins parcourent les océans, et
dans les forêts, l'angoisse, la douleur et la mort remplissent
l'air. Il y a une seule chose qui manque dans ce monde
souterrain: le ciel avec ses éclairs et son soleil. Le Talmud est
comme ce monde sans ciel. Il est immense mais il nous
enchaîne à la terre. Il ne nous permet pas d'oser chercher
d'autres mondes. Mais le Kabbale ravit l'âme et la transporte
au palais céleste.

(*Train sound in the distance. Chirp freeze.*)

DAVID: (*In relief that he's still alive.*) Shema Yisroael, adenoi
elohanu, adenoi echod.

ESTHER: (*As MESSENGER. Dragging the action back.*) And
then the fiancé arrived. (*She puts a hat on JAN.*)
Menache with his father Nachman. (*She puts a hat on
DAVID.*)

DAVID: But I'm Hanan.

RACHEL: Hanan just died. Remember.

ESTHER: Everyone has to play several roles. Now you are
the prospective father-in-law.

DAVID: (*Reluctantly taking a different hat.*) I only want to
play Hanan.

ESTHER: (*As MESSENGER. Forcing DAVID to play NACHMAN
and JAN to play MENACHE.*) The journey was difficult.
The journey was difficult…

DAVID: (*As NACHMAN.*) The journey was difficult. We got
lost and wandered around for hours in the fields. Then we
fell in a marsh. I began to wonder if certain spirits were
interfering with my journey. But, thank God, here we are.

NAOMI: (*As SENDER.*) You must be tired. Rest a while.

DAVID: (*As NACHMAN.*) No, there isn't time. We've still got
to discuss more about the dowry and the presents. (*He
takes JAN/MENACHE aside.*) Don't move. Don't even look
up. Keep quiet. Understand?

JAN: (*As MENACHE.*) I understand. I'm frightened. I've
been terrified ever since we left our house. There's an
Evil Eye here. I'm frightened and most of all by that girl.

DAVID: (*As NACHMAN.*) Don't worry. God will protect you.

NAOMI: (*As SENDER.*) Let's go to the inn. We'll eat there.
(*As BEGGAR. Grotesque movement.*) They promised us all
a full plate and they've given us next to nothing.

RACHEL: Stick to the story.

NAOMI: I am doing. Now I'm one of the beggars at the
marriage.
(*As BEGGAR.*) They said we'd leave with full bellies. But
me, I can't move for the gurglings inside. My stomach
begins to eat itself.

DAVID: Look at that man eating bread.

ESTHER: The more they eat, the more there is for the
worms. Come on, let's get the wedding over with.
(*The group make a chuppa/wedding canopy from ladders.
JAN/MENACHE is pushed under the chuppa with RACHEL/
LEAH. He tries to kiss her. She rejects him.*)

RACHEL: (*As LEAH.*) You're not my fiancé.
(*LEAH and a MALE DANCER perform the Dance of Death.
The Dance symbolises the invasion of the dybbuk into LEAH's
body.*)

RACHEL: (*As LEAH/DYBBUK.*) You may have buried me
but I have come back. I have returned to she who is my
destiny and I will never leave her.

NAOMI: (*As SENDER.*) She's gone mad.

ESTHER: (*As MESSENGER.*) Enter the great Rabbi Azriel.
(*She puts a hat on DAVID.*) He is eating after sabbath with
his students.

NAOMI: Always eating.

DAVID: Yes, I like to play the rabbi.

DAVID: (*As RABBI.*) I'm going to tell you a story. One day
a group of clowns arrived from Germany. They threw
a cord over a river and then proceeded to cross the
river, tightrope. All the village came out to watch this
marvellous event. Suddenly, amidst the crowd, they
noticed the great man Baal Shem Tov. 'What are you
doing here,' they asked. 'I wanted to watch a man walk

across the abyss,' he said. 'If a man can work on his soul
as purposefully as he works on his body then what
spiritual abyss can he cross on the delicate thread
of life.'

RACHEL: (*As LEAH/DYBBUK.*) I am wronged. I am
wronged.

NAOMI: (*As SENDER.*) Rabbi, my daughter. She is ill. With
a dybbuk. Help me please.

DAVID: I am weak and tired. I am tired of the sins of men.
Their sins are like arrows in my flesh.

ESTHER: Come on, we've got to finish it.

NAOMI: (*As SENDER.*) Have pity on me. My only daughter.

DAVID: (*As RABBI.*) How did she get this dybbuk?

NAOMI: (*As SENDER.*) I don't know.

RACHEL: (*As LEAH/DYBBUK.*) Liar.

NAOMI: (*As SENDER.*) Lelele!
Rabbi. My daughter is pious and pure.

DAVID: (*As RABBI.*) There has to be a worm first to corrupt
the flesh.
(*During this NAOMI packs her case ready for deportation,
even though she still speaks SENDER's words.*)

NAOMI: (*As SENDER.*) Rabbi, I don't know.

DAVID: (*As RABBI.*) Sometimes the children are punished
for their parents' sins.

NAOMI: (*As SENDER.*) If I'd sinned I would have begged
forgiveness.

DAVID: (*As RABBI.*) Have you asked the dybbuk why he has
entered this poor girl's body? Did you know him?

NAOMI. (*As SENDER.*) He dined at our table.

DAVID: (*As RABBI.*) Did you offend him?

NAOMI: (*As SENDER.*) I don't know. I don't think so.
Rabbi, I'm only a poor man.
(*DAVID/RABBI lifts the unwilling RACHEL/LEAH onto
the 'acting' platform.*)

DAVID: (*As RABBI.*) Enter Leah.

RACHEL: (*As LEAH.*) I cannot.

DAVID: (*As RABBI.*) I order you to enter.

RACHEL: (*As LEAH.*) Leave me alone. I don't want to.
(*She tries to run, the others stop her.*)

DAVID: (*As RABBI.*) Dybbuk, who are you?

RACHEL: (*As LEAH/DYBBUK.*) Zadik of Miropol. You know who I am.

DAVID: (*As RABBI.*) It's not your name I need but your spirit.

RACHEL: (*As LEAH/DYBBUK.*) I am one of those who seek new paths.

DAVID: (*As RABBI.*) Only he who has lost the right road moves towards the crossroads.

RACHEL: (*As LEAH/DYBBUK.*) The straight road is too narrow.

DAVID: (*As RABBI.*) The words of the Fallen Angel. Dybbuk. Why have you entered this young girl?

RACHEL: (*As LEAH/DYBBUK.*) She is my chosen one.

DAVID: (*As RABBI.*) A dead man is not allowed to be among the living.

RACHEL: (*As LEAH/DYBBUK.*) I am not dead.

DAVID: (*As RABBI.*) You have left our world and it is forbidden to return until the trumpets sound for the Last Judgement. Dybbuk, I order you to leave the body of Leah.

RACHEL: (*As LEAH/DYBBUK.*) Rabbi of Miropol. I know of your power. You can order the angels and the cherubs. But not me. Where would I go? All the roads are closed to me. There is heaven and earth, there are worlds without end.
(*As herself.*) England, America, Africa. But nowhere, nowhere is there a space for me

NAOMI: (*Carrying her suitcase, waiting for deportation.*) Oh God, there is no space for us. No space for us.

RACHEL: (*As LEAH/DYBBUK.*) I have found my resting place here. Don't chase me away.

DAVID: (*As RABBI.*) Lost soul, I feel for you most deeply but you must leave the body of this young girl. D-y-b-b-u-k out!

RACHEL: (*As LEAH/DYBBUK.*) I won't go. N-o-o-o-o-o-o-o...

DAVID: (*As RABBI.*) D-y-b-b-u-k out!

RACHEL: (*As LEAH/DYBBUK.*) No. I won't go.

DAVID: (*As RABBI.*) Dybbuk out!!!!

RACHEL: (*As LEAH/DYBBUK.*) No!!!!!!!!!!!!!!!!!!!!!!!!!!!!!!!!!!!!!
(*Loud crash as the Nazis arrive to take them for deportation
to Auschwitz.*
They throw themselves into each other's arms.
Blackout.
*Very high volume sound of banging smashes the action. The
transport from the ghetto.*
Trains sound.
*Mozart's Mass in C Minor (the Lachrymosa) mixed with
Hitler's speeches, dogs, guns.*
*A corridor of light through which the actors enter in a stylised
movement sequence.*
*They walk through one by one. At first with looks of horror,
then with defiance, at times they walk through in groups,
carrying a dead comrade on their back or in their arms.*
A woman carries two men, a man carries a man, etc.
*The movement must be perpetual, symbolising the murder of
six million but the effect must be of death and rebirth.*
You can kill a people but you cannot kill their culture.
*Very slow blackout so that the falling and returning remain
as an after-image.*
During the blackout the actors leave.
*Hold sound of Mozart during slow lights up to stage filled
with battered cases, coats, hats, playing cards and books.*
*Fade out sound and leave the audience looking at the relics of
those just murdered.*
Silence.)

The End.